PAPER + Pixels
Scrapbook Layouts

May Flaum & Audrey Neal

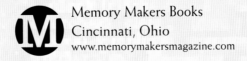

Memory Makers Books
Cincinnati, Ohio
www.memorymakersmagazine.com

12 11 10 09 08   5 4 3 2 1

Distributed in Canada by Fraser Direct
100 Armstrong Avenue
Georgetown, ON, Canada L7G 5S4
Tel: (905) 877-4411

Distributed in the U.K. and Europe by David & Charles
Brunel House, Newton Abbot, Devon, TQ12 4PU, England
Tel: (+44) 1626 323200, Fax: (+44) 1626 323319
E-mail: postmaster@davidandcharles.co.uk

Distributed in Australia by Capricorn Link
P.O. Box 704, S. Windsor, NSW 2756 Australia
Tel: (02) 4577-3555

Library of Congress Cataloging-in-Publication Data
Flaum, May.
  Paper + pixels : scrapbook layouts / May Flaum and Audrey Neal. -- 1st ed.
      p. cm.
  Includes index.
  ISBN 978-1-892127-93-8 (pbk. : alk. paper)
  1. Photographs--Conservation and restoration--Data processing. 2. Photography--Digital techniques.
3. Photograph albums--Data processing. 4. Scrapbooks--Data processing. 5. Digital preservation. I.
Neal, Audrey. II. Title.
TR465.F635 2008
771--dc22
                          2007033263

F+W PUBLICATIONS, INC.

Editor: Kristin Belsher
Designers: Kelly O'Dell, Anne Shannon, Corrie Schaffeld
Art Coordinator: Eileen Aber
Production Coordinator: Matt Wagner
Photographer: Tim Grondin
Stylist: Nora Martini

www.fwpublications.com

Check out the authors' blog at www.paperandpixels.vox.com for updates, challenges and other fun extras.

about the authors

May's Story

I am a lifelong paper crafter, and for a long time, I resisted the lure of digital scrapbooking. Then about two years ago, some of my friends started doing some pretty cool things with Photoshop. I also started to find some amazing digital papers and embellishments. In other words, my "not me, never" stance started to weaken. I found myself wondering if I could harness the power of the digital realm and channel it into my paper world.

Turns out, I could. For me, paper crafting is the ultimate hobby, and scrapbooking is my greatest passion. I can capture moments, preserve history, and it serves as a wonderful artistic outlet. Creating albums as gifts is a great part of the process. Thanks to digital techniques and products, I have been able to create one-of-a-kind pages and bring some of my wildest visions to paper.

I dedicate this book to my friends and family who have given me love, support, and helped to make this dream come true. Especially my husband, daughters, and my mom.
—May Flaum

DIGITAL SUPPLIES:
Paper by Mary Ann Wise (Designer Digitals); brushes by Jason Gaylor (Designfruit); image editing software (Adobe)

TRADITIONAL SUPPLIES:
Decorative tape, flower (Heidi Swapp); chipboard accent (Scenic Route); letter stickers (Creative Imaginations, K&Co.); ribbon (May Arts); decorative scissors; buttons, charm, tag (unknown); pen

Audrey's Story

I live in a pretty computer-savvy household. My husband and I each have our own computers, as well as a variety of peripherals and software. I'm comfortable with a number of programs and don't have any problem teaching myself something new. So you'd think I'd be an old hand at using digital techniques. Not so. My pages were de-cidedly low-tech for years: I journaled in my own handwriting, and my pictures were straight from the camera. I swore I'd never go digital. I thought digital pages were too slick, too flat, too graphic. I liked inked edges, torn paper and lots of funky texture.

Then I found the online scrapbooking community and fell in love with the work of several scrapbookers. As I browsed their galleries, I noticed digital elements. So I tried my hand at a digital page, and then another, and another. Before I knew it, I was hooked. I had gone over to the dark side, as a friend put it. And I'm so glad I did. Do I call myself a digital scrapbooker now? No. But I don't call myself a paper scrapper or a hybrid scrapper either. I'm just a scrapbooker who uses a variety of tools and techniques to tell my stories.

I dedicate this book to the daily reminders that I already have everything I'll ever need: Chris, Cass and Cami; and to the memory of my father, Virgil Clark.
—Audrey Neal

DIGITAL SUPPLIES:
Grid paper from Touch of Funk kit by Kim Christensen; glitter splotches, stars, watercolor paper by Tracy Ann Robinson (Scrapbook Bytes); image editing software (Adobe); Porcelain font (Internet donwload)

TRADITIONAL SUPPLIES:
Transparent letters (Heidi Swapp); brads; ink; pen (Sakura)

table of contents

Digital scrapbooking stirs up a lot of mixed emotions in scrapbookers. Some people love it, while others hate it. There's a third group as well—the ones who just aren't sure. They don't want to give up their paper supplies, but they're curious to see what all this digital fuss is about. They're teetering on the edge of experimentation, waiting for the right push to send them over.

So why haven't they jumped in yet? There are so many reasons. Most graphics programs have a fairly high learning curve, which intimidates many scrapbookers. Others fear that the expense will be too great, and still others feel they don't have the time to devote to learning new techniques. The list could go on.

That's why we've come together to create this book, to show you quickly and easily how to combine digital products and paper techniques to create exceptional pages. From paper to pixels, we'll guide you into the digital world and show you how to bring some of that technology back home to your paper scrapbook pages.

Getting Started:
Technology + Materials

iBook

Sometimes the most daunting aspect of getting started is actually getting started. Learning something new can be overwhelming and leave you wondering where to begin. That's where this section comes in! Before you dive into the lessons, take some time to read through the following pages. Find out about the hardware essentials, software basics and potential materials to use. Our advice is this: Take it step by step and enjoy the journey.

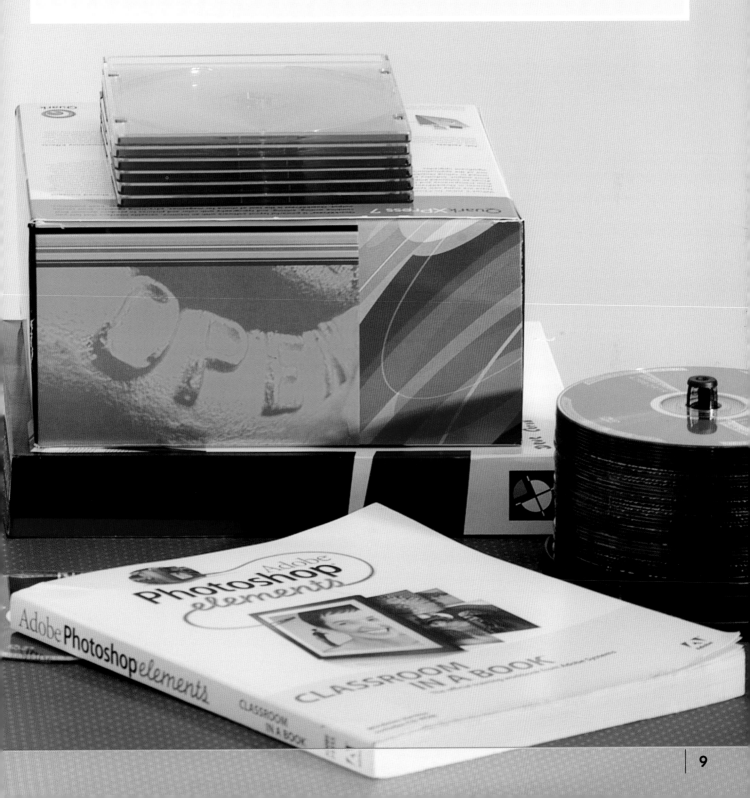

defining hybrid scrapbooking

The world is full of famous pairs: Peanut butter and jelly. Salt and pepper. Ben and Jerry. Now you can add digital scrapbooking and traditional scrapbooking to the list. After all, using both techniques offers the best of both worlds, combining the flexibility of digital technology with the tactile appeal of paper crafting.

Sadly though, hybrid scrapbooking, because it's so closely related to digital scrapbooking, is widely misunderstood in the scrap world. To put it simply, hybrid scrapbooking means using your computer software (whether it's a word processing program, photo-editing software or a full-out graphic design program) to create some aspect of your page design. Truth be told, you're probably already doing some hybrid scrapbooking. You want examples? Adding a border or text to your photos before printing is hybrid scrapbooking. Creating a title with WordArt is hybrid scrapbooking. Printing digital papers is hybrid scrapbooking. See where we're heading with this? Hybrid doesn't mean going completely digital. You can use as many or as few digital elements as you want. And this book is your chance to learn to use even more.

What's most exciting about hybrid scrapbooking, for us, is that you don't have to change your style or method of scrapbooking to embrace it. If you enjoy using paint and inks to get messy and artsy, you can keep doing that. But why not use your computer to print a cool image onto a transparency and then trim it to create your own stencil? If you enjoy adding doodles to your page, scan some of your drawings and then change them to brushes in Photoshop. Want to mimic lumpy, textured pages without taking up so much space in your albums? Digital embellishments can give you the look—just print them out.

Take a look at the next page, which illustrates how digital elements serve to enhance a paper page. Before long, you'll be completely convinced that hybrid scrapbooking really is as good as peanut butter and jelly.

A Traditional Layout

A paper page employs a number of dimensional items for texture and variety. Layered papers, chipboard accents, ribbons and brads all give the page a tactile appeal.

Audrey Neal

TRADITIONAL SUPPLIES:
Patterned paper (Dream Street); chipboard letters, transparent frames and word (Heidi Swapp); chipboard arrow (Fancy Pants); rub-on journaling block (Hambly); ribbon (American Crafts); brads (Junkitz); pen (Sakura); sketch by Nicole White

A Digital Layout

A page can be assembled quickly with a digital kit, and coordinating is simple. And like a paper layout, an entirely digital page uses layers and elements like patterns and embellishments. But when printed, digital layouts lack the real dimension that paper scrappers desire.

May Flaum

DIGITAL SUPPLIES:
Papers, embellishments by Katie Pertiet (Designer Digitals); Marcelle Script font (Internet download); Miss Johnson font by Tia Bennett Two Peas in a Bucket)

A Hybrid Layout

This page shows how well digital and paper elements can come together on a page. To create this page, I printed the two papers (red and dotted) along with the bottom swirl on one sheet. I printed other elements and inked them for dimension. I added traditional embellishments, such as rhinestones and chipboard, to enhance the basic page design. As you can see, a hybrid page puts the computer to use while still providing a tactile experience.

Audrey Neal

TRADITIONAL SUPPLIES:
Cardstock (Bazzill); chipboard letters, rhinestones (Heidi Swapp); letter stickers (Making Memories); rub-on bird (American Crafts); ink (Colorbox); pen (Sakura)
DIGITAL SUPPLIES:
Paper (red, dot) and bird by Holly McCaig (My Digital Muse); graph paper by Gina Cabrera (Digital Design Essentials); swirls by Lauren Reid (ScrapArtist)

hardware

Implementing new digital techniques sometimes means dealing with loads of new equipment, user's manuals, software upgrades, and accessory packages. But you don't have to have a roomful of cutting-edge computer hardware to get started with hybrid designs. The equipment you've got is probably plenty. At the least, you'll need a computer and a printer. A scanner isn't necessary for most of the techniques we'll teach you, but it does make a great addition to your basic hardware set.

Keep your computer specifications in mind when using image-editing programs like Adobe Photoshop Elements or storing digital photographs and scrapbooking kits. The minimum recommended specifications for running Photoshop Elements include 256MB of RAM (memory), 1.5GB of available hard drive space (storage) and an Intel Pentium 4 or Intel Celeron (or compatible) 1.3 GHz processor. That's not to say that older computers won't run the program; my processor is only half the recommended size, and I'm still able to run Photoshop Elements with ease. The only real issue is that some tasks, such as applying filters, take additional time to complete on older machines.

We frequently hear people claim they can't use digital techniques because they don't have a wide-format printer. That's just not true. You can create gorgeous hybrid 12" x 12" (30cm x 30cm) pages with nothing more than a letter-sized printer. In fact, about half the 12" x 12" (30cm x 30cm) layouts in this book were created using a standard printer. Of course, we love the freedom a wide-format printer gives you to create papers, overlays and more on a 12" x 12" (30cm x 30cm) page.

Two additional tools will enhance the use of hybrid techniques discussed in the lessons. A digital camera makes it easy to manipulate photos with a photo-editing program. Graphics tablets, such as those made by Wacom, also give you more opportunity to explore the world of design.

storage + organization

Of course, stepping into the digital realm means more than just having the right hardware. You need a place to store all your digital elements. Although there are several image organization software programs available, we like to take advantage of Windows Explorer, since it comes installed on your PC.

There are numerous ways to store your photos and digital supplies, but let us share how we do it. We keep all our photos in one folder (on a designated drive) labeled "Photos" or "My Pictures." Inside that folder, we create a series of additional folders, one for each month. As we upload and rename our photos, we move them to the appropriate monthly folder. We suggest including the date in the name of each photo. If you're ambitious, you can take this several steps further and create more folders within each monthly folder—perhaps you want to label them according to event or person. Once each month is complete, we move that folder to a folder labeled with the year. At the end of the year, all of the photos from the previous 12 months will be stored and organized, and we'll be ready to start the process over for a new year.

We use a similar organizational method with our digital kits, although, you've got several options that will work effectively for this task. You can create a folder for each digital designer, so that you can easily go to a designer's kit. You can also store kits according to theme, color scheme, or by store. We suggest that you keep kit components together in the folder they come in, rather than splitting them up into other categories. When you split your kits, it's harder to remember who made what, which is important for proper crediting if you submit your layouts or post them in online galleries.

To make it easier to identify kits, we suggest you save the preview and set it as the image on the front of the kit's folder. To do this, right click on the folder and select Properties. Select the Customize tab, then select Choose Picture. Navigate to your desired photo and double click on it. Select Apply, then OK, and close the dialog box. You can also store each kit preview in a separate folder marked "Previews" so that it's easy to choose a kit.

Above all, we urge you to experiment with finding a system that works best for you. One of the most important things to remember is to always back up your files. At the end of every month, burn that month's photos to a CD or DVD. Do the same with your digital purchases for the month. Do a second backup to an external hard drive as well. As the old saying goes, it's better to be safe than sorry!

Digital kits carry with them a different set of "rules" for use than most scrapbooking supplies. When you purchase a package of eyelets or some sheets of cardstock, once you've used them, you can't reuse them. Digital supplies, on the other hand, can be used over and over again. As a result, digital kits will come with a set of rules, called a Terms of Use (TOU). This document, which is usually a text file contained within your downloaded kit, will outline what you can and can't do with the digital kit. For example, you can't share a downloaded kit with friends or family. This is piracy and is unethical. Most digital kits can't be used for commercial purposes, which means you can't modify and then resell the kit's contents. It's important to respect the TOU of digital supplies, and if ever in doubt, ask the designer.

Equally important to remember is that your traditional scrapbook supplies have rules, as well. Scanning your papers and embellishments to create digital files should never be done.

*materials

One of the most exciting things about incorporating digital techniques into your paper pages is the range of media available for printing. You're not limited to photo paper or cardstock; in fact, you're not even limited to paper at all! Here's a list of some of our favorite materials to print on.

* Photo papers come in a wide variety of types, including high gloss, soft gloss or satin, and matte. It's advisable to use the same brand of paper as your printer to ensure optimum compatibility and print quality. You'll find that with some experimentation, different types of papers yield different results. We prefer matte paper because it's less likely to smudge or smear and doesn't show print lines like some glossier papers do. But it's ultimately a matter of finding the paper you like.

* Cardstocks come in a number of textures and thicknesses. We've found that non-textured cardstock and lightly textured cardstock hold a slight edge over more heavily textured stocks, which often lose fine detail during printing.

* Transparencies have become a popular scrapbook supply because of their flexibility. With transparent sheets, you can make custom transparent frames and letters and create cool effects for your photos. Some lighter colors are less visible on transparencies, so back them with light-colored paper for better readability.

* Fabric papers, such as canvas, silk, and organza types, are backed with paper so you can easily feed them through your printer. Attach them to your design with stitching, brads, eyelets, staples or fabric glue. For a less visible bond, try using fusible webbing. Fabric paper is a great way to add texture to your pages.

* Vellum and other specialty papers also can be used for layering and texture. Be sure to do a test print first, so you can see how long the ink takes to dry, and check the print quality before using an entire sheet. Delicate papers, such as mulberry and rice paper, should be adhered to a sheet of standard printer paper with removable or repositionable adhesive before printing. You can also use this technique to print on some varieties of ribbon and twill.

* Sticker paper and labels are fantastic for creating personalized stickers, journaling boxes, and other embellishments. They're primarily available in white or clear, but you can find some colored versions as well.

A few final points to remember: Always follow the manufacturer's directions when using any specialty printing products. Buy paper designed for your type of printer (laser or inkjet), and adjust your printer's settings as needed for the best print possible.

*programs

We'll be using two programs in the lessons throughout this book: Microsoft Word and Adobe Photoshop Elements. Word offers an easy way to become acquainted with hybrid scrapbooking. Because it's likely already a part of your computer's software package, it can be a familiar means of learning new digital techniques. Photoshop Elements is a popular image-editing software program and provides a wide variety of tools for creating hybrid scrapbooking pages. Before you begin the lessons, take some time to read the program overviews below to familiarize yourself with the programs' basic set-ups and commands.

Microsoft Word

Word is the standard in word-processing software. With its intuitive user interface and dropdown menus, it makes creating text-based documents a painless experience. The versatility of the program makes it useful for altering and creating images as well. While Word lacks many of the more sophisticated tools found in programs intended for graphic design, its basic tools can be put to a variety of creative and clever uses on your scrapbook pages. Although you're probably pretty familiar with the ins-and-outs of Word, we want to remind you of some basic commands as well as some that might be unfamiliar.

After opening Word, you'll be greeted with this basic screen:

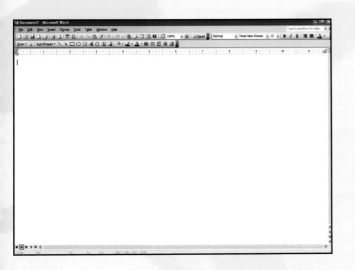

Your main menu is located along the top left of your screen, with shortcut icons on the toolbar directly below that. Spend a few minutes browsing through the commands in the menu to reacquaint yourself with what's available. If you have a question about any command, use the Help feature (F1).

Several of our lessons require you to use additional toolbars—mostly the Picture and Drawing toolbars. To view these toolbars, go to View>Toolbars.

The Picture toolbar consists of 14 icons. From the left, they are Insert Picture, Color, More Contrast, Less Contrast, More Brightness, Less Brightness, Crop, Rotate, Line Style, Compress, Text Wrapping, Object, Set Transparent Color and Reset Picture.

The Drawing toolbar contains 16 icons. From the left, they are: Line, Arrow, Rectangle, Oval, Insert Text Box, Insert WordArt, Insert Clip Art, Insert Picture, Fill Color, Line Color, Font Color, Line Style, Dash Style, Arrow Style, Simple Shadow and 3D.

Here are a few more basic commands that you'll need to know to successfully complete the lessons.

* To open a new document, go to File>New, or click on the blank page icon in the standard toolbar.

* To open an existing document, go to File>Open, or click on the file folder icon.

* Right-clicking on an object brings up a shortcut menu, which provides you with cut, copy and paste options, as well as options for formatting, grouping and ordering.

Adobe Photoshop Elements

Photoshop Elements allows you to make adjustments to digital photos, as well as add graphics, create brushes, type fancy text, and much more. This program may take a while to get the hang of, but once you're familiar with the menus and options, it's straightforward to operate. There are currently five versions (1.0-5.0); the older versions don't have as many features as the newer ones. Lessons in this book refer to version 4.0, but most can be applied to any of the Photoshop Elements versions.

If you're just starting to explore digital design and have not yet used Photoshop Elements, allow yourself some time to get to know the program. There's a lot to learn with this program, so it's best (and least frustrating!) to start simple.

When the program is open it will look like this:

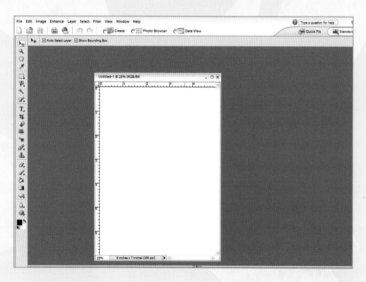

Note the toolbar on the left-hand side of the screen. This holds your basic tool icons. From top to bottom, the tools are: Move, Zoom, Hand, Eyedropper, Marquee, Lasso, Magic Wand, Selection Brush, Type, Crop, Cookie Cutter, Red-Eye Removal, Healing Brush, Clone Stamp, Pencil, Eraser, Brush, Paint Bucket, Gradient, Custom Shape, Blur and Sponge. Clicking on the tool name provides a pop-up help screen explaining the tool. When you select a tool, a new toolbar appears across the top of the screen. For example, if you click on the Text tool, the text toolbar opens, providing options like font size and color.

For the lessons in this book, you will frequently be using the Move, Text, Crop and Brush tools.

Along the top of the screen there's a menu of choices that allows you to open files, create new files, enhance photos, add filters, and more. We will explain some basic commands here, and many of these will also be covered in the lessons.

✳ To open any photo, digital element, or other file go to: File>Open.

✳ When creating a new file, go to File>New>Blank File; you will have many options. You can choose the size of the file, resolution, color mode and background color. Unless otherwise noted, when creating a new file for a lesson, choose 300 dpi, RGB color, and transparent background.

Finally, we need to take a moment to discuss layers. In paper scrapbooking you bring together multiple layers of photos, embellishments, papers and other elements. Until you glue them down, you can move them around and change the order as much as you like. Keep this in mind when working in Photoshop. Every time you add another element to your digital file, you're adding another layer. By using the move tool, you can resize and move the individual layers. Using the Layer menu (at top right of screen) and the Layer palette (to the right) you can create new layers, merge layers together, duplicate layers, and more.

Above all, enjoy the learning process. You'll be a Photoshop Elements expert in no time!

For Mac Users

The keyboard shortcuts that we've included in the lessons are for Windows users. If you're a Mac user, the chart below will help you find the equivalent shortcuts for your program:

PC: Ctrl = Mac: Command
PC: Alt = Mac: Option
PC: right-click = Mac: <Ctrl>+click

*about the CD-ROM

You'll find a CD loaded with 12 fabulous digital kits tucked in the back of this book. The kits feature a variety of designs and styles, with numerous papers, embellishments, letters and other elements to add to your pages. We've included elements from some of these kits in our own layouts, so you'll have the opportunity to work with the kits in the lessons. Visit the Gallery of Ideas to see how the contributors put the kits to use. Throughout the book, you'll see the 💿 icon each time a kit from the CD is used.

Authentic Me
By Lauren Reid

Bloom
By Tracy Ann
Robinson

Flowering Horizons
By Katie Pertiet

Perfect Summer
By Jackie Eckles

Seriously Pink
By Poppy Andrews

Sweet Baby Chic
By Michelle Coleman

Touch of Funk
By Kim Christensen

Unconditional
By Jen Wilson

Vagabond
By Jan Crowley

Welcome Home
By Lynn Grieveson

Template Kit
By Jen Caputo

Template Kit
By Janet Phillips

Let Digital
Do It for You:
Lessons

We've put together 40 step-by-step lessons for photos, text, papers and embellishments. Divided into beginner, intermediate and advanced levels, these lessons provide you with a toolbox of techniques for creating hybrid pages. Use these techniques individually or combine them for more intricate designs. Regardless of how you use them, we're confident you'll be creating gorgeous hybrid designs in no time.

Part 1 | Photographs

For as long as I (Audrey) can remember, I've loved to look at photographs. My grandparents had a large white faux leather album with gold edges and an embossed gold script on the front. It sat on the bottom shelf of the sofa end table, and no visit to my grandparents' house was complete without a look through the album. Most of the photos were formal portraits of my mother and her sisters, as well as my grandparents and their parents. I vividly recall the weight of the album as it rested on my lap, my legs sticking straight out in front of me on the floor.

Scrapbooking has changed the way we create albums, but the essence of those afternoon sessions spent flipping through my grandmother's album remains the same. Our photos are the heart and soul of our albums, regardless of their format or size. Technology has brought a new element to scrapbooking, and it's providing many scrapbookers with an easy way to improve their photography skills so they can capture more memories. The popularity of digital cameras means that many of us scrapbookers want to use image-editing software to touch up or alter our photographs. In addition to basic uses, such as color conversions and lighting fixes, there are many ways to alter your photographs so they not only tell your story well but also accent your pages with fresh new designs.

Glossary of Photography Terms

Brightness: the lightness or darkness of a color, also called value.

Contrast: the range of value in an image (from black to white); a low-contrast photo consists mainly of similar gray values, while a high-contrast image covers a wider range of values from black to white.

Opacity: the transparency of an image; the less opaque an image is, the more visible items behind it become.

Saturation: the richness or intensity of a color.

The following lessons provide step-by-step instructions for both common and creative photo techniques. Be sure to check out the Gallery of Ideas on page 108 for more examples of ways to digitally enhance your photographs.

Lesson 1:
Editing Photos | Beginner

Audrey Neal

My daughters spend as much time as possible in the inflatable pool, and I'm guaranteed to capture their best smiles during those times. To create this layout, I printed a strip of black and white photos. I kept the document open after printing, noting where the last two photos were placed. I deleted the photos and inserted the quotation in their place. I loaded my photo strip back into the printer (making sure it would print the same direction) and printed. Then I traced the text with a glaze pen. I cut the photo strip and attached it to a large piece of polka-dot cardstock. I printed the focal point photo in color, matted it on patterned paper and tore the edge, then attached it over the photo strip with foam adhesive. I added strips and blocks of patterned paper. After printing it, I cut the journaling into strips, attached it with brads, and finished by adding plastic and rub-on letters.

DIGITAL SUPPLIES:
Quotation from Perfect Summer kit by
Jackie Eckles ✸ A Little Pot font (Internet download)

TRADITIONAL SUPPLIES:
Patterned paper (Scenic Route); plastic letters (Heidi Swapp); rub-on letters (KI Memories); corner rounder; brads (Junkitz); glaze pens (Sakura); adhesive foam (Therm O Web); adhesive (Beacon)

Photos with lots of reflected light—such as those taken on water or snow—can have exposure problems. Although Word isn't considered a photo-editing program, it does include a few tools that let you make minor changes to your photographs.

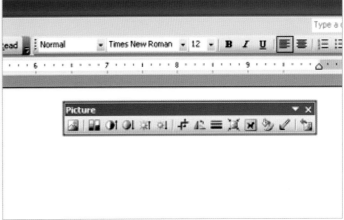

1 To maximize your work space, go to File>Page Setup and adjust the margins to .5" (13mm). Also change your page orientation to landscape. To insert your photo, choose Insert>Picture>From File, then navigate to the proper drive and choose your photo. Click Insert to drop the photo on the page. Click on the picture to make the Picture toolbar appear on your screen.

2 Use the Picture toolbar to adjust the brightness and contrast of your photo. Click on the sunshine icons (to adjust brightness) and the black and white circle icons (to adjust contrast). The up arrows increase brightness and contrast, while the down arrows reduce brightness and contrast. These buttons can be used to adjust the brightness and contrast of both color and black-and-white photos.

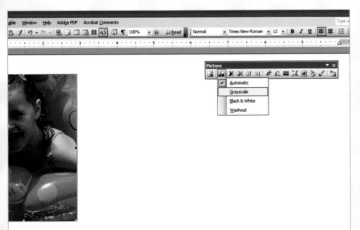

3 To make your photo black and white (also called grayscale), select the Color option on the Picture toolbar and choose Grayscale.

4 To create a row of photographs, size one photo to your desired measurements. Then copy and paste the picture three times without hitting <return> after each paste. You can space the photos by using the space bar between each photo.

Note: If you want to start over during an adjustment process, simply click the Reset Picture icon, located at the right end of the Picture toolbar.

Lesson 1:
Editing Photos | Intermediate

May Flaum

We all have those pictures that recall wonderful stories and memories but that didn't turn out so well. With the help of Photoshop, I was able to improve my Christmas Eve photos, creating a layout that perfectly captures the memories, one that I'm proud to show off. To create this page, I assembled pieces of patterned paper over background cardstock and rounded the corners. I edited the photos and printed them. I then attached the photos over the patterned paper and added a chipboard title outlined with white pen. To complete the layout, I attached rub-on images, twill and journaling tags, then added journaling.

DIGITAL SUPPLIES:
None

TRADITIONAL SUPPLIES:
Cardstock; chipboard letters, patterned paper (Scenic Route); rub-on accents (Fancy Pants); die-cut label (Daisy D's); stamp, twill (Autumn Leaves); corner rounder; ink (StazOn); pen (Sakura)

We all have photos that hold dear memories but are flawed with red eyes or bad lighting, or are in need of cropping. Photoshop Elements allows you to correct and improve your photos in many ways.

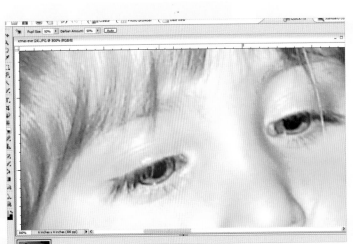

1 Once your photo is open, select the crop tool. To set an exact size, make adjustments in the menu (in the crop toolbar) before cropping. Use the crop tool to highlight the area you want to crop. You can move or resize the crop borders by clicking on them. Hit <enter> to accept the crop. (Note: Hitting <esc> will undo your highlighted crop selection.)

2 To remove red eyes, start by zooming in (using the zoom tool) so your subject's eyes are large and you can see the pixels that need to be changed. Then select the red eye removal tool. A small + will appear; use this to select the areas from which to remove red eye.

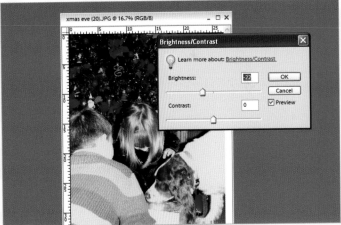

3 There are several ways to make a photo black and white. An easy way is to use Image>Mode>Grayscale. If you want a bit more control, go to Enhance>Adjust Color>Adjust Hue/Saturation. When the menu opens, you can adjust the saturation on your photo as desired. (Note: Using -95 to -100 percent saturation will make a photo grayscale. To make a photo appear faded, try - 75 to -90 percent saturation. There are many other color adjustments you can make in this menu.)

4 You can find most of the color-editing tools for basic corrections in the Enhance menu. To change a photo's brightness or contrast go to Enhance>Adjust Lighting>Brightness/Contrast and adjust the settings as needed.

Note: If you aren't comfortable adjusting levels of saturation and brightness and want a quick fix, the Auto Levels option (Enhance>Auto Levels) often produces a satisfactory effect. Remember, if you don't like the results, you can just click on the backward arrow to undo them.

Audrey Neal

Program:
Microsoft Word

New technique:
Using the Picture toolbar to
reduce a photo's opacity

Skills you'll need:
Adjusting page orientation (p. 23)
Inserting photos (p. 23)

Downtown Paducah, Kentucky, is a thriving historic district in the midst of some incredible renovations. One of my favorite things to do is to walk around taking photographs of the buildings. To create this layout, I layered strips of patterned paper onto a cardstock base. In Word, I created a photo collage with three photos (using reduced opacity on two), printed them, matted them onto cardstock, and attached them to the page. I adhered ribbon and another strip of paper over the top of the layout. Then I attached chipboard letters on patterned paper, embellished the letters and added them to the page along with a journaling block. Finally, I printed a quotation on a transparency and attached it with brads.

DIGITAL SUPPLIES:
Café Rojo font (Internet download)

TRADITIONAL SUPPLIES:
Cardstock (Worldwin); patterned paper (Imagination Project, Mustard Moon); chipboard letters (Heidi Swapp); ribbon (Strano); brads (Paper Studio); rhinestones (My Mind's Eye); transparency; adhesives (Beacon, Therm O Web); pen (Sakura)

Placing text on top of your photos can create a sophisticated look with depth and dimension. Sometimes, however, a photo's bright colors can make this a difficult look to achieve. Reducing a photo's opacity is one way to put text over an image while keeping the photo intact.

1 Adjust the margins and page orientation of a new document, and insert your photo. To resize your photo, click on the photo so that the adjustment handles appear in the corners. Place your cursor over a corner handle, hold down your left mouse button, and drag your cursor toward the opposing corner. Use the rulers at the top and left of your screen as a guide.

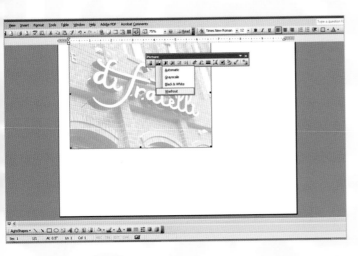

2 To reduce the opacity of your photo, go to the Picture toolbar, click on the color icon (the black and white bars) and choose Washout. If you feel you've lost too much detail with this selection, adjust the brightness and contrast until you achieve the desired look.

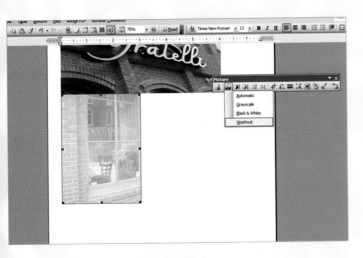

3 You can create a photo collage using the techniques described above with three photographs: one horizontal and two vertical. Insert the horizontal photo into a new document, resizing it to approximately 6″ (15cm) wide. Hit <return> and insert the second photo. Resize it to approximately 3″ (8cm) wide and reduce the opacity. Insert the third photo, resize it to 3″ (8cm) wide and reduce the opacity.

Changing Color and Opacity | Intermediate

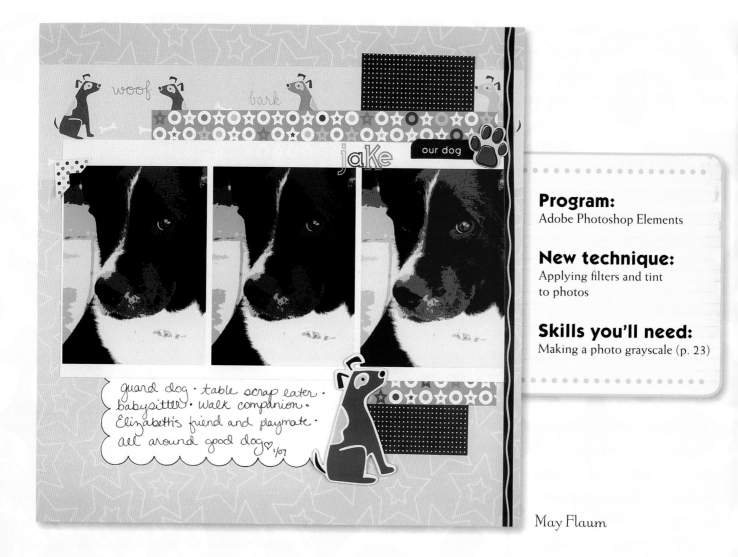

Program:
Adobe Photoshop Elements

New technique:
Applying filters and tint
to photos

Skills you'll need:
Making a photo grayscale (p. 23)

May Flaum

It's important to me to include my furry family member on my scrapbook pages, so I decided to use a favorite new photo to try out an artistic effect. This layout is not only fun but also simple and quick to create. To make this layout, I first edited photos and created a digital collage. I printed the collage on photo paper, trimming excess paper as needed. I cut large strips of patterned paper and assembled them over a sheet of patterned cardstock. I attached the photo collage on top of the paper then added a piece of scalloped cardstock with journaling. Finally, I added stickers and embellishments.

DIGITAL SUPPLIES:
None

TRADITIONAL SUPPLIES:
Cardstock (Bazzill); chipboard accents, letter stickers, patterned paper, sticker accents (KI Memories); pen (Sakura)

Making different versions of a favorite photo allows you to create a dynamic layout. You can use the Filter Gallery in Photoshop Elements to create all sorts of artistic photo effects with ease.

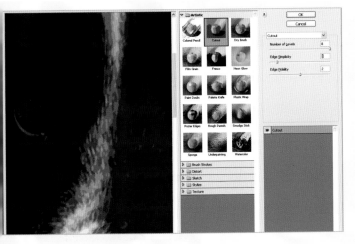

1 First, open a photo and make it grayscale. Then go to the Filter Gallery (Filter>Filter Gallery). Here, you can preview various artistic effects and adjust the intensity they'll have on your photo. (I used the cutout feature in the Artistic menu.) Once you're satisfied with the look, select OK. Then resize your photo to about 3.5" x 4.5" (9cm x 11.5cm).* To resize, go to Image>Resize>Image Size.

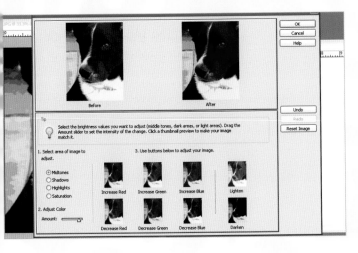

2 Create an 11" x 8.5" (28cm x 22cm) blank file (New>Blank File). Select the move tool, then click on your photo and move (drag) your photo into the blank file. To create tinted versions of a photo, return to the photo in the first file. From the Enhance menu, go to Color>Color Variations. Adjust the color and intensity as desired and select OK. Move the photo into the new 11" x 8.5" (28cm x 22cm) file next to the grayscale version.

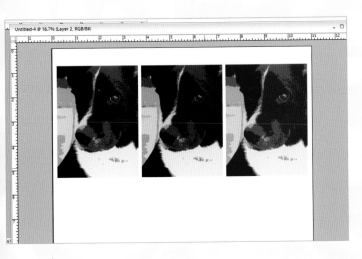

3 Return to the first photo again. Click the backward arrow to undo the color tint. Then repeat the steps above to give the photo a new tint (e.g., red). Drag the new photo into the 11" x 8.5" (28cm x 22cm) file, and place it to the right of the other two photos.

*All measurements in this book are listed as width first, then height. For example, a document listed as 8.5" x 11" (21.5cm x 28cm) indicates the size is 8.5" (22cm) wide and 11" (28cm) high.

Lesson 3:
Creating Photo Collages | Beginner

Program:
Microsoft Word

New technique:
Resizing and moving
photos to create a collage

Skills you'll need:
Adjusting page orientation (p. 23)
Inserting photos (p. 23)
Resizing photos (p. 27)

May Flaum

I love getting out early on a spring morning and photographing the flowers in my garden. To celebrate that feeling, and the simple beauty of the flowers, I created this page. I began this layout by creating a photo collage in Word, printing it onto white photo paper and trimming it around the edges. I then attached a piece of patterned paper to a sheet of background cardstock and attached the photo collage to the patterned paper. Next, I added a chipboard title, stickers, and ribbon strips to the page and adhered flowers and embellishments on top of the ribbons. I stamped a floral image onto cardstock, colored it with glaze pens, cut out the image with pinking shears and attached it to the page. To complete the look, I attached a lace swan and added journaling.

DIGITAL SUPPLIES:
None

TRADITIONAL SUPPLIES:
Cardstock (Prism); chipboard letters, patterned paper, sticker accents (Creative Imaginations); ribbon (Heidi Grace, May Arts); twill (Autumn Leaves); flowers (K&Co., Prima); brads (K&Co.); stamp (Art DeClassified); swan accent (unknown); ink (StazOn); pen (Sakura)

To create a collage of odd-sized photos, as well as to save time, I often print multiple photos on one sheet of photo paper and use the whole page in my layout design. Word makes this quick and easy to do.

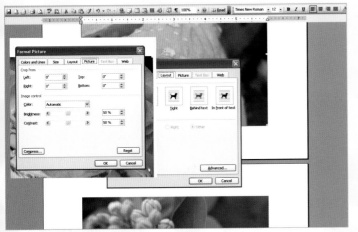

1 Adjust the margins and page orientation in a new document, and insert your photographs. You can select more than one photo by holding down <ctrl> when selecting. After opening, format the photos using the Picture toolbar or the Format Picture menu. To open the Format Picture menu, double-click on the picture. Be sure to resize photos using the corners of the picture; this keeps the photo proportions correct.

2 Once the photos are ready, you can arrange them on the page. To move a photo easily, go to the Format Picture menu. Click on the Layout tab and choose "In front of text." Exit the menu, and drag the photos around the document as desired.

Another Great Idea!

You can use the same techniques described above to create a collage like the one Audrey made here. Insert your first photo, resizing it as needed to fit three on the page vertically. Hit <enter> to move to the next line, and insert another photo. Repeat these steps with a third photo, and check that all three are touching at the top and bottom edges before printing the page. Then print a large photo as tall as your layout. Cut a circular edge on the photo, then layer it over the photo collage to give the collage a rounded edge.

DIGITAL SUPPLIES:
Papers by Katie Pertiet, Flowering Horizons kit; Bahia Script SSK, Vianta fonts (Internet download)

TRADITIONAL SUPPLIES:
Cardstock (Die Cuts With A View, Worldwin); lace (Fancy Pants); buttons (Autumn Leaves); photo corner (Deluxe Designs)

Audrey Neal

May Flaum

Program:
Adobe Photoshop Elements

New technique:
Using a pre-made template to create a photo collage

Skills you'll need:
Moving photos (p. 29)
Locating the Layers palette (p. 16)

The first trip to Disneyland with my daughter was a big deal. I had hundreds of photos, laughs and memories that I wanted to preserve. To start my album, I wanted to create an opening layout that had tons of photos from the vacation. I used a digital template to arrange my photos and printed the photo collage on two sheets of 12″ x 12″ (30cm x 30cm) cardstock, setting the printer for borderless printing. To embellish the page, I added a bit of journaling, rub-ons, stickers and chipboard.

DIGITAL SUPPLIES:
Page template by Anna Aspnes (Designer Digitals)

TRADITIONAL SUPPLIES:
Cardstock (Prism); chipboard letter and accents, glitter rub-ons (Cloud 9); letter stickers (Doodlebug, Heidi Grace, Making Memories); heart and word rub-ons (Heidi Grace); pen (Sakura)

Pre-made templates for Photoshop Elements are widely available for purchase on digital scrapbooking Web sites. Templates make it easy to create complex photo collages that showcase all your favorite photos.

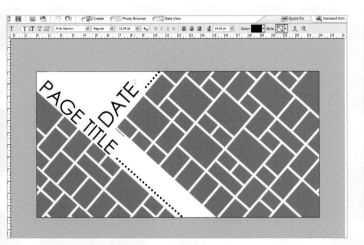

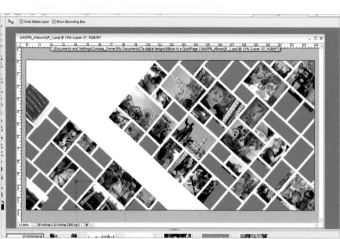

1 Open a downloaded template as you would an image file. To change the title text on the template, select the text tool, highlight the title, delete the text and type your own title. (I chose to delete the title and create my own using letter stickers.)

2 Open a few of your photos at a time, formatting them to sizes appropriate for placing in the template. Move the photos into the template file. To move a photo in front of or behind another, click on the photo's layer in the Layers palette and hit <ctrl+[> (move back) or <ctrl+]> (move forward). Continue placing photos until the template is complete. Then merge the layers (Layer>Merge Visible) so you can move the whole template.

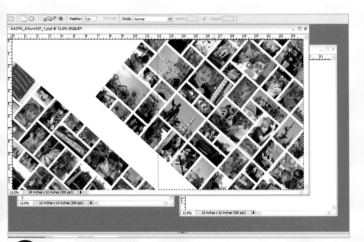

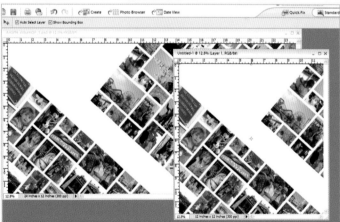

3 If your template is 24″ x 12″ (70cm x 30cm), you need to print it in two parts. Open two new files, each at 12″ x 12″ (30cm x 30cm). Select the rectangle marquee tool. Place your cursor at the top right corner of the template. Drag your mouse until the marquee (dashed) square reaches 12″ x 12″ (30cm x 30cm); use the screen ruler as a guide. Then, using the move tool, drag the area in the marquee square onto the blank file. Print the page.

4 To print the second page, select the marquee tool again, this time choosing the area to the left of the page. Then use the move tool to drag the selected area onto the other blank 12″ x 12″ (30cm x 30cm) file and print.

Note: Going to Layers>Merge Visible merges all the layers in a file including the background (also called "flattening"). This is best used when you're finished formatting a file.

Lesson 4:
Adding Brushes, Frames and Photo Masks
Beginner/Intermediate

May Flaum

Program:
Adobe Photoshop Elements

New technique:
Adding brushes and frames
to a photo

Skills you'll need:
Resizing images (p. 29)
Moving images (p. 29)
Locating the Layers palette (p. 16)
Merging all layers (p. 33)

I wanted to create a page that represented my current style and place in life. To soften the look of this photo and to complement the page's overall design, I used digital brushes and frames in addition to decreasing the saturation of the photo. After adding a digital frame to the photo, I printed it on photo paper. I cut various patterned papers in different sizes, assembled them on the page and then added the photo. To create the title, I stamped a script stamp onto chipboard letters and edged them with a silver leafing pen. While that dried, I journaled on a piece of lined paper and attached it to the page. I attached the title and added rub-on designs, buttons, a flower and other accents.

DIGITAL SUPPLIES:
Brush and frames by Katie Pertiet (Designer Digitals)

TRADITIONAL SUPPLIES:
Cardstock (Prism); patterned paper (Autumn Leaves, BasicGrey, K&Co.); journaling paper (Creative Imaginations); chipboard letters (Scenic Route); rub-on accents (BasicGrey); stamp (Art DeClassified); ink (StazOn); flower (Prima); buttons (Autumn Leaves); metal accents (Nunn Designs); pen (Sakura); silver leafing pen (Krylon)

Adding digital brushes and frames to photos can create unique focal point photos. Opacity adjustments allow you to layer and blend these elements seamlessly for a soft and sophisticated look.

1 Open your photo and edit as needed. (I desaturated mine 75 percent.) Click on the Brush tool and select a brush from the Brush toolbar. Adjust the brush's opacity and color (using the Brush toolbar). Options like adjusting the angle of a brush can be changed by clicking on the More Options button. Stamp the brush around the edges of your photo.

2 Open a decorative frame image in a new file. Resize it (as you would a photo) so it's close to the size of your photo. Drag the frame onto your photo and adjust the size more, if needed.

3 Select the frame layer in the Layers palette. Choose the Eraser tool, and select a large, round brush. Adjust the opacity as desired. While holding down your mouse button, sweep the eraser over the entire frame. Do this in one motion to create a smooth brush stroke. (Note: Only the frame should be erased because that's the layer you selected. If something else is erased, the wrong layer is selected. Hit Undo, select the frame layer, and try again.)

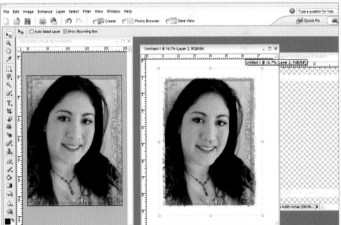

4 Merge all the layers. Create a new 8.5" x 11" (22cm x 28cm) file and drag the image into the blank file. Open a grunge frame (in white) and resize the frame to the size of the photo. Drag the frame into the new file, placing it around the photo so the photo's edges become rough. (I have found that a good kit of digital grunge frames and overlays is well worth the cost.)

Note: If your brush selection menu doesn't include the brush you want to use, you can load a brush. Go to the brush selection menu, click the fly-out menu (the arrow pointing right) and choose Load Brushes.

Lesson 4:
Adding Brushes, Frames and Photo Masks | Advanced

Program:
Adobe Photoshop Elements

New technique:
Changing the shape of a
photo using a photo mask

Skills you'll need:
Resizing images (p. 29)
Moving images (p. 29)
Selecting layers (p. 35)

Audrey Neal

DIGITAL SUPPLIES:
Take Two photo masks by Tracy Ann Robinson
(Scrapbook Bytes); Brushstrokes brushes by
Michelle Coleman (Little Dreamer Designs);
Journaling Brushes-n-Stamps brushes by Katie
Pertiet (Designer Digitals); Polaroid 22 font
(Internet download)

TRADITIONAL SUPPLIES:
Cardstock (Paper Studio); brads, patterned paper
(Around the Block); transparency (Grafix);
adhesive (Beacon); pen (Zig)

Printing onto transparencies is one of my favorite tricks, so when I started this layout, that's pretty much all I had
in mind. I thought it would be interesting to layer a few digital elements over some brushes. After playing around,
here's what I came up with. To create this page, I cut a piece of patterned paper to 8.5" x 11" (22cm x 28cm) and tore
white cardstock to fit across the center of the page. In Photoshop, I created a photo collage, adding a photo mask
to soften the edges. I also added digital paint strokes to the top and bottom corners of the collage, and added a blue
title and blue journaling brackets to the collage. I printed the collage onto a transparency and placed it over the
white cardstock. Then I printed a close-up photo and slipped it behind the edge of the title.
I added brads to the page and journaled with a permanent marker to finish.

While frames and brushes are designed to be placed on top of a photo, photo masks are designed to be placed under a photo, so the photo takes on the shape of the mask. This is a different way to create "frames" for your photos.

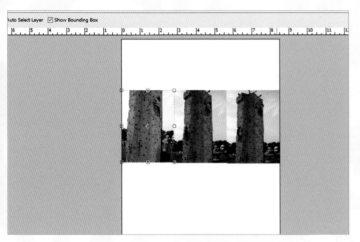

1 Open a new 8.5" x 11" (22cm x 28cm) file and open a new layer (Layer>New Layer). Insert your first photo; go to File>Place and choose your photo file. Resize the photo to roughly 2.75" (7cm) wide. Repeat these steps with two more photos. The photos should extend from one side of the page to the other. Merge just those three layers (but not the background). To do so, hit <ctrl> and in the Layers palette, select the layers you want to merge. Then hit <ctrl+E> or go to Layers>Merge Layers.

2 Open the file with your photo mask and move the mask into the photo file. Place the mask on top of the photos and resize the mask until the pictures are just covered. In the Layers palette, drag the photo mask layer underneath the photo layer. To do this, click on the photo mask layer, and, while holding the mouse button down, drag it up or down the list of layers until it's just below the photo layer.

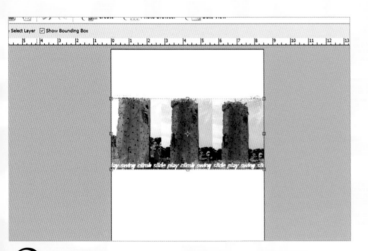

3 Select the photo layer and clip it to the photo mask layer by hitting <ctrl+G>. (Note: Clipping one layer to another causes the selected layer to take on the shape of the layer beneath it.) Make any adjustments to the size or position of the photo layer, then merge it with the mask layer.

Defining Decorative Elements:
Brushes, Overlays, Frames and Photo Masks

Think of **brushes** as stamps for Photoshop. You can resize them and "stamp" them on your layout. Photoshop comes with a variety of brushes, but you can buy them from digital designers online or create your own. **Overlays** can take on a variety of appearances, including patterns and grungy designs. It's common to layer an overlay over a digital paper to change its appearance, often giving the paper a textured look. **Frames** are the simplest way to add visual interest to photos. Frames are available in a variety of styles. **Photo masks** can add decorative edges to your photos. Masks are available from a variety of digital designers.

Lesson 5:
Extracting Photos | Beginner/Intermediate

Audrey Neal

Program:
Adobe Photoshop Elements

New technique:
Creating photo silhouettes by using the Lasso tool and removing color

Skills you'll need:
Moving photos (p. 23)
Adjusting contrast (p. 25)

My youngest daughter is the spunkiest thing I've ever seen. She's just got one of those personalities that reaches out and grabs you. Needless to say, it shines through in her photographs. To create this layout, I staggered four silhouetted images across patterned cardstock. The first image was relatively small and had an opacity of 40 percent. For each additional image, I increased the opacity by 20 percent and the size by about 1" (3cm). I inked the edges of both layers of cardstock, then printed title blocks and a journaling label, and inked those edges as well before adhering them to the page. I painted chipboard swirls and journaled on top of them after they dried. To embellish the page, I added rhinestone flowers and glitter glue.

DIGITAL SUPPLIES:
Heart accent, label, letters and patterned paper from Seriously Pink kit by Poppy Andrews

TRADITIONAL SUPPLIES:
Cardstock (Die Cuts With A View); brads (Making Memories); rhinestones (Heidi Swapp, unknown); chipboard swirls (Deluxe Designs); acrylic paint (Delta); ink (Clearsnap); adhesive (Beacon); pen (Sakura)

Creating silhouettes and making color adjustments can add a creative and funky touch to your page designs.

1 Open your photo and move it into a blank file. Make any necessary corrections and adjustments. Next, select the Magnetic Lasso tool. While holding down your mouse button, trace the object that you want to cut out. Release the mouse button when you're back at your starting point. The object in your photo should now be surrounded by blinking dashes, which indicate that you have that area selected.

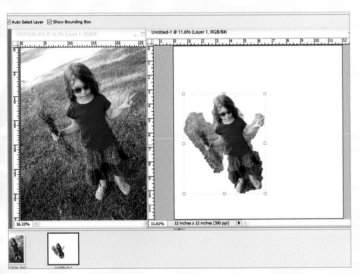

2 Right-click on your image and select Layer Via Copy. Then open a blank 12″ x 12″ (30cm x 30cm) file with a white background. Drag the selected area in your photo onto the blank file.

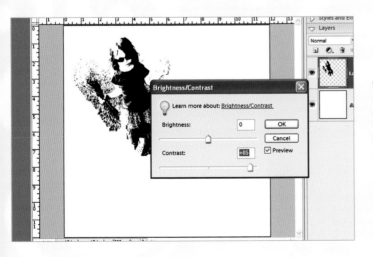

3 To change an image to only black and white (as opposed to grayscale, which uses black and white, as well as shades of gray) go to Enhance>Adjust Color>Remove Color. Adjust the image's contrast as needed. (I set my image's contrast to 85.) Repeat the process to create three more silhouetted images in the same file. Adjust the opacity (in the Layers palette) and size as desired.

Lesson 5:
Extracting Photos | Advanced

Jason and me, getting ready to whoosh down the mountain at Northstar (Tahoe). Well... the truth is that Jason's friend took this photo of him getting ready to head down a black diamond slope while I struggled with the tiny trainee ski slope. This was my first (and last) ski trip, and it was a lot harder and scarier than I anticipated. To be honest I don't think I'll be doing it again anytime soon. However thanks to Photoshop Elements I was able to insert myself into this cool mountain top photo can pretend that I am great at skiing... if only in my mind.

Snow Day

January '04

May Flaum

Program:
Adobe Photoshop Elements

New technique:
Using the Lasso tool to blend two photos

Skills you'll need:
Moving photos (p. 29)
Resizing photos (p. 29)
Using the Lasso tool (p. 39)
Selecting layers (p. 35)
Erasing images (p. 35)

I naively thought skiing would be easy and that I'd get several chances to "swoosh" down the slopes with my husband. Like many things in life, it wasn't that simple, and I never did swoosh successfully. My husband and I never got a photo together at the top of the mountain, so I decided to take a humorous approach to this layout and blend two photos together with the help of Photoshop Elements. To create this layout, I edited and printed a blended photo. I then typed my journaling and printed it on a piece of cardstock. I cut the paper to size and inked the edges. I cut pieces of patterned cardstock, inked those edges, and adhered them along with the journaling to a large sheet of patterned paper. I added rub-ons, brads and chipboard snowflakes. To complete the page, I applied rub-on letters.

DIGITAL SUPPLIES:
Sailboat font (Two Peas in a Bucket)

TRADITIONAL SUPPLIES:
Cardstock (Prism); patterned paper (BasicGrey, Scenic Route); rub-on letters (Scenic Route); ribbon (BasicGrey); brads, snowflake accents (Autumn Leaves); photo corners (unknown); ink (Ranger)

Using tools such as the Lasso, Selection Brush and Eraser, you can blend two or more photos in unlimited ways.

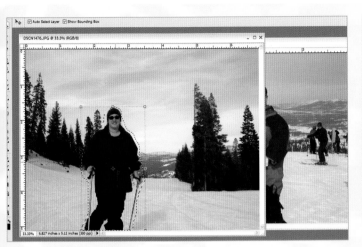

1 Open the photos you want to blend together and drag the photos into separate new files. Resize the photos to the same size. Then use the Lasso tool to select the part of one photo you want to transfer to the other.

2 Drag the selected area onto the other photo. Place the new layer as desired.

3 Select the layer with the imported area and erase the parts of the area that you don't want to keep. If you want softer edges, change the eraser's opacity level or select a soft brush. If you want to be very exact in erasing portions of the imported area, zoom in closely so you can see exactly which pixels you're erasing.

4 If you're satisfied with the placement of the imported photo, your work is done! But you can also make part of the background photo appear to be in front of the imported portion. To do so, open the original background photo, and with the Lasso tool, select the area you want to place in front of the imported area. Drag the newly selected area onto your blended photo and position it. Erase any pixels that you don't want.

Part 2 | Text

The text on your scrapbook pages can set the mood, enhance the story and bring more life to your photos. Your computer increases creative possibilities and allows you to make artistic and customized designs.

In this chapter, we explain various ways to create text using Word and Photoshop Elements. From creating text boxes to using brushes and effects, this chapter is bursting with ideas for producing decorative text.

The first thing you need in order to create interesting text is an assortment of fonts. Your computer already includes at least a few fonts, but there's a vast selection of fonts available on the Internet, both free and for purchase. (See the source guide at the back of this book for Web site information.) If you're like us, you'll become totally addicted to fonts and all the great text effects you can create. (You've been warned!)

Before we get started with the lessons, here are a few helpful hints for using text:

- To change font, size, spacing, color and other options in Word, go to Format>Font. You can also use the toolbar along the top of your screen, or you can highlight the text, right-click and select Font.

- In Photoshop Elements, when you have the text tool selected you can change the font, size, alignment and more by using the text toolbar along the top of your screen.

- When choosing a font for journaling, remember that simple is best. Fancy, embellished and intricate fonts are better suited for titles and other large text.

A few of our favorite journaling fonts:

Bookman Old Style   (Microsoft)

Garamond (Microsoft)

A Beautiful Mess (Two Peas in a Bucket)

A Little Pot

Vaguely Repulsive

Lesson 1:
Creating White Text | Beginner

Audrey Neal

Program:
Microsoft Word

New technique:
Using text boxes to create white text

Skills you'll need:
Resizing images (p. 27)

I ended up with so many pictures of my family throughout the year that I wanted to display some of them in a way that would give an overview of what our year was like. The song "Seasons of Love" from the Broadway musical *Rent* has always been a favorite, so pairing that with a calendar-type layout was a great choice. To create this page, I made a table in Word (with 24 cells) and printed it onto white cardstock. I placed the table on top of scalloped cardstock and then layered sheets of patterned paper underneath. I created and printed colored text boxes and trimmed them with decorative scissors to echo the shape of the scalloped cardstock. I then printed small photos, attached them to the layout, and added embellishments and title letters to complete the page.

DIGITAL SUPPLIES:
AL Songwriter font (Two Peas in a Bucket)

TRADITIONAL SUPPLIES:
Cardstock; patterned paper (Paper Salon); chipboard letters, flowers (Heidi Swapp); rub-on letters (CherryArte); brads (Bazzill, Paper Studio); decorative scissors; corner rounder; adhesive; pen (Uniball, Zig)

You might not be able to print in white ink, but you can certainly fake the look by creating text boxes in Word. Once you've learned this versatile trick, printing in white is easy!

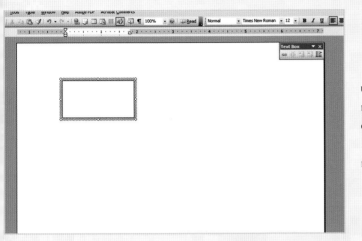

1 Open a new document. To insert a text box, go to Insert>Text Box. A cross will appear in place of the cursor; use that to draw a text box on your screen by holding your right mouse button and dragging your cursor toward the bottom right corner of your screen. Make the text box roughly 2″ x 1″ (5cm x 3cm). (Note: Using the corner handles to resize the text box will maintain its orignal proportions.)

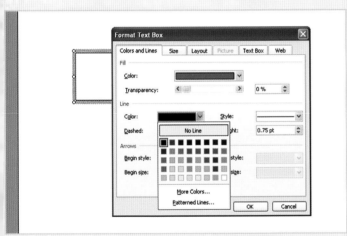

2 To format the text box, right-click on the border of the box, and select Format Text Box from the options that appear. (You can also click on the text box and go to Format>Text Box.) To fill your text box with a color, click on the arrow next to Color and select a color. If you want to customize your color, select More Colors and use the Standard or Custom tools to create a new color. If you want a border around your text box, make the necessary color and weight adjustments in the Line menu. If you don't want a line, select No Line.

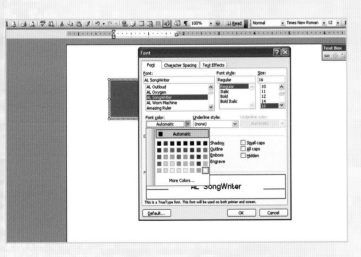

3 To add white text to your text box, first select a font and size from the Font menu (Format>Font) or the Formatting toolbar (at the top of the screen). Set white as your font color. Then place your cursor inside the text box and type your text. Resize your text box (as you would an image) if it's too small to fit the text. You can also adjust the font size to fit the text in the text box. To center text in the box, use the text alignment tools in the standard toolbar at the top of your page.

Lesson 1:
Creating White Text | Intermediate

Program:
Microsoft Word

New technique:
Using text boxes and WordArt to create a layered design with white text

Skills you'll need:
Inserting new text boxes (p. 45)
Formatting text boxes (p. 45)
Resizing text boxes (p. 45)
Formatting text (p. 45)

Artist in training

Not even two years old, and you are already totally into art. It is so much fun to watch you experiment, explore, and enjoy paints, crayons, pens, stamps, and any other art supplies we'll let you have. I hope that you continue to love arts and crafts the way that I do throughout your life.

October 2006

May Flaum

Art is such a joy of mine, and it makes me so happy to see my daughter already enjoying her creative time. I wanted a playful, slightly messy look for this page to make it feel as fun as possible. To create the page, I first made the title and journaling text boxes in Word and printed them onto cardstock. Then I randomly stamped the background cardstock with a dot stamp and metallic paint. (It's OK to be a bit messy sometimes!) Next, I assembled scraps of patterned paper, journaling and photos on the page. To complete the layout, I added ribbons, rub-ons, chipboard and a metal accent.

DIGITAL SUPPLIES:
Brandywine and Freestyle Script fonts (Internet downloads)

TRADITIONAL SUPPLIES:
Cardstock (Prism); chipboard accents, patterned paper (Imagination Project); rub-on accents, tag (BasicGrey); bookplate, stamp (Junkitz); ribbon (Strano); dot accent (Cloud 9); paint

Now that you can create white text and text boxes, try adding dimension by layering multiple text boxes and WordArt.

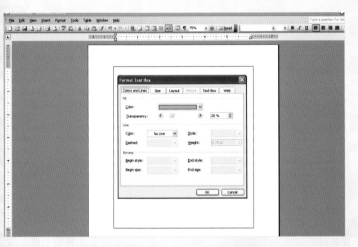

1 Open a new document and begin by inserting a new text box. Format the text box to the size and color you want the background box to be (this box is blue on my layout), and select No Line. Insert another new text box, resizing it smaller than your first box. Fill it with a coordinating color (I used purple) and select No Line. Move the second text box over the first, as needed. To move a text box, click on its border and drag with your mouse.

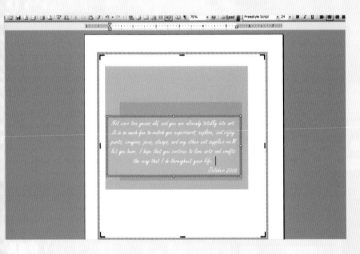

2 Insert a third text box to house your journaling, resizing it to fit the text. Also be sure to choose a color that makes white text readable. Move the third text box over the first two.

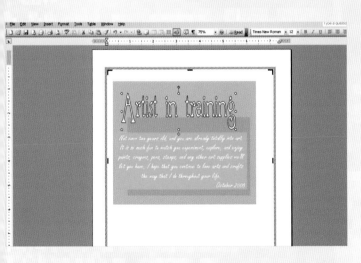

3 You can add a title to the collection of text boxes, using WordArt. Go to Insert>Picture>WordArt. In the WordArt gallery, choose the option that shows white text outlined in black. Type your title in the box and choose a font style and size. Move the WordArt to your desired location and resize it, as needed. (Note: See Lesson 3 in this chapter for detailed WordArt instructions.)

Note: When inserting additional text boxes into a document, be sure to click outside of (deselect) any existing text boxes. If a text box is selected when inserting another, the new text box is inserted inside the existing box.

Lesson 2:
Layering Text | Beginner

To live in this world,
you must be able to
do three things:

to love what is mortal,

to hold it
against your bones
knowing

your own life
depends on it,

and when the time comes
to let it go,

to let it go.
-- Mary Oliver

Audrey Neal

Program:
Microsoft Word

New technique:
Layering text boxes to produce layered text effects

Skills you'll need:
Inserting new text boxes (p. 45)
Formatting text boxes (p. 45)
Resizing text boxes (p. 45)
Formatting text (p. 45)
Moving text boxes (p. 47)

This is one of my favorite poems, and fall is my favorite time of year. I thought the poem would complement the mood of these photos, and using my favorites made for a personal page that I really enjoy. To create this page, I first overlapped text boxes in Word and then printed the poem on cardstock. I layered the poem, along with my three photos, over plaid paper, then inked the edges. To create the leaf embellishments, I created a series of text boxes and used the Fill Effects option to add patterns and color to them. I printed them on vellum and sprinkled them with embossing powder before the ink dried completely. I heat embossed the vellum, traced the cardstock leaf shapes onto the vellum, then cut them out and adhered them to the cardstock shapes. I glued the leaves to the layout and added ribbon and tabs.

DIGITAL SUPPLIES:
AL Worn Machine font (Two Peas in a Bucket); Eight Fifteen font (Internet download)

TRADITIONAL SUPPLIES:
Cardstock (Bazzill); patterned paper, tab (Piggy Tales); vellum; ribbon (Strano); fabric tab (Scrapworks); chipboard (Deluxe Designs); embossing powder; ink; adhesive

Text boxes make layering text a cinch! Use the technique to highlight words, add dimension and produce creative effects for even your simplest pages.

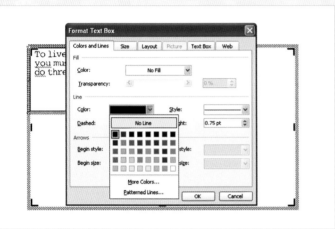

1 Insert a text box into a new document. Type your text in the text box and resize it to fit the text. Adjust the font size, style and color as desired; for lots of text, choosing a basic font in a small size (about 14 point) is best. Format the text box using the Format Text Box menu, making sure you have No Fill and No Line selected.

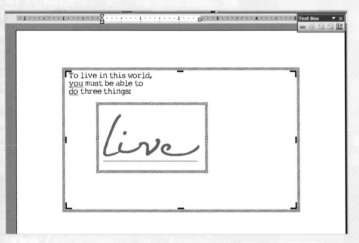

2 Insert a second text box into your document. Format the text box, selecting No Fill and No Line. Choose a more decorative font in a large size for this second text box. Also choose a very pale version of the color used in your original text box. Type your text into the box.

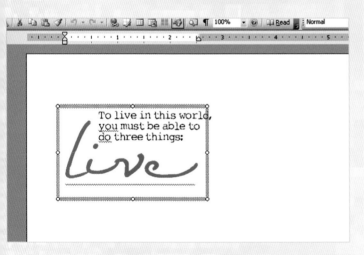

3 Move your second text box so that it's very near or slightly overlapping your original text. You can use the Order function (right-click on the border of the text box and select Order) to move one text box behind or in front of another. Repeat this process with other text and key words as desired.

Lesson 2:
Layering Text | Intermediate

Program:
Adobe Photoshop Elements

New technique:
Using the Text tool to produce layers of decorative text

Skills you'll need:
Resizing images (p. 45)
Merging select layers (p. 45)

May Flaum

I can taste the sweet strawberries just looking at these photos! To create this layout, I digitally layered a title over my photo of strawberries in Photoshop. I printed that and an additional photo, allowing for white borders on both. I then used a black pen to outline the letters in the word Strawberries. I layered several sheets of patterned paper and attached the photos to the paper. I finished by attaching die-cut labels for journaling and adding ribbon and flower accents.

DIGITAL SUPPLIES:
Floral paper from Welcome Home kit by Lynn Grieveson 🌸; Doodlesticks font (Two Peas in a Bucket); Girls are Weird and Santa's Sleigh fonts (Internet downloads)

TRADITIONAL SUPPLIES:
Cardstock (Prism); patterned paper (K&Co.); die-cut labels (Daisy D's); ribbon (KI Memories); embroidered flower accents (unknown); pen (Sakura)

The possibilities for designing layered titles in Photoshop are only limited by your imagination. The layered titles you create can be used alone or placed over photos and digital papers.

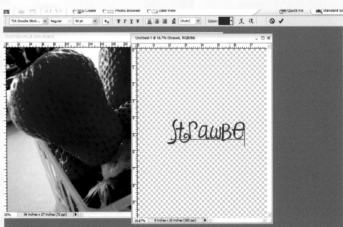

1 Open the photo over which you will place your title. Then open a new transparent file. Be sure to make your new file bigger than your title will be. Begin by selecting the Text tool and choosing a font color. To select a color that matches your photo, go to the text toolbar, and click on the Color box to open the Color Picker. Hold your mouse over the photo to make the Eyedropper tool appear. Select a color from your photo by clicking on it.

2 Type one of your title words. To move the text, use the Move tool. Resize the text the same way you would other images. You can change the font or color of the text by selecting the Text tool and changing your selection in the text toolbar.

3 To create the next layer of text, simply select the Text tool and click in any blank space in the file. Change the font and text color as desired, and type the next word(s) in your title. Resize and move the text into place. Repeat this step for any additional text layers.

4 Once your title is complete, merge just the text layers so you can move them onto the photo. Drag the title from its file to the photo file. If needed, you can move and resize the title to fit.

Lesson 3:
Creating Decorative Titles
Beginner/Intermediate

May Flaum

Program:
Microsoft Word

New technique:
Using WordArt to create
decorative titles

Skills you'll need:
Inserting photos (p. 23)

Crafting pages about my husband's work is important to me, and I jumped at the chance to photograph him in the dress uniform I see only twice a year. To create this page, I made a WordArt collage in Word and printed it on cardstock. I then printed my photos (after changing the saturation to -75 percent) and assembled them with the WordArt and patterned paper on a cardstock background. I paperclipped my journaling to the page to add dimension, and attached photo corners and ribbon. Then I embellished the page using brads and rub-ons.

DIGITAL SUPPLIES:
Bookman Old Style font (Microsoft); Brandywine, Marcelle Script and Scriptina fonts (Internet downloads)

TRADITIONAL SUPPLIES:
Cardstock (Prism); patterned paper (Mustard Moon, Scrapworks); ribbon, rub-on accents (BasicGrey); note paper, transparency frame (My Mind's Eye); photo corners (Heidi Swapp, KI Memories); brads; paper clip; pen (Sakura)

Using WordArt in Word allows you to add multiple text layers in a variety of styles to provide more creative formatting for your layouts.

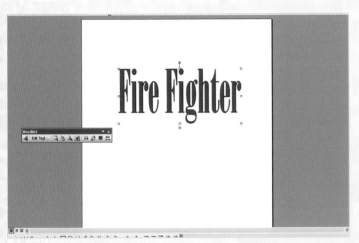

1 After opening a new document, go to Insert>Picture> WordArt. Choose a style of WordArt from the gallery. Type your text, choose a size and font, and click OK. The WordArt should now be placed in your document, and a small toolbar should be visible. The WordArt toolbar allows you to change any WordArt setting—including text shape, size and color—at any time.

2 Continue creating WordArt using various font sizes and styles. Holding the mouse button down over WordArt text allows you to move it, and using the handles you can to adjust the size. You also can move WordArt in front or in back of other objects by right-clicking on the WordArt and selecting Order.

3 To place a photo behind your WordArt, insert a photo into the document. If needed, move the photo behind the WordArt using the Order function.

4 After inserting the photo, you may find that some text does not show up well. Simply click on the WordArt and use the WordArt toolbar to change the font, color or size.

Lesson 3:
Creating Decorative Titles | Advanced

Audrey Neal

Program:
Adobe Photoshop Elements

New Technique:
Using brushes to create decorative titles

Skills you'll need:
Cropping photos (p. 25)
Moving images (p. 29)
Resizing photos (p. 29)
Using the Brush tool (p. 35)
Clipping layers (p. 37)
Merging select layers (p. 37)
Merging all layers (p. 33)

Photos with large amounts of white space, an area free of images and text, provide a unique opportunity for including decorative titles and journaling blocks on a page. To create this layout, I added the title and snowflake images to a digital photo before printing. Then I placed my photos and blocks of patterned paper onto large sheets of cardstock. I coated chipboard snowflakes with glitter glue and attached them to a ribbon border with rhinestone brads. Then I added more sparkle with rhinestone shapes. A printed journaling block finished the page.

DIGITAL SUPPLIES:
Snowflake brushes by Rhonna Farrer (Two Peas in a Bucket); decorative text (Jen Wilson)

TRADITIONAL SUPPLIES:
Patterned paper, chipboard snowflakes (Autumn Leaves); rhinestones (Heidi Swapp); snowflake accents (Me & My Big Ideas)

Photos by Kim Hendricks

Adding digital drawings—often called dingbats—and brushes to titles is a great way to emphasize your theme and liven up a page.

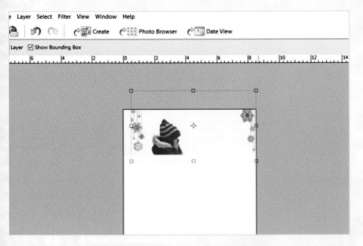

1 Open a new letter-sized file. Then open up your photo in another file. (Note: Choose a photo that has a large amount of white space, e.g., a snowy landscape, an empty sidewalk, or a blank wall.) Crop your photo so it retains its original width but is only 1.5″ to 2″ (4cm-5cm) tall. Drag the photo into your blank file; resize the photo as needed so it covers the width of the file. Close the original photo file.

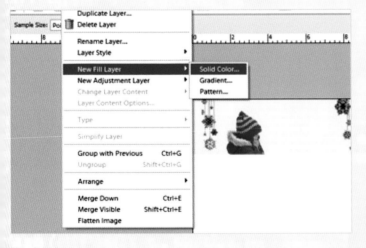

2 Choose a brush to add to the photo. Stamp the brush in a new layer. Your brush will probably be black. To change the color, make sure your foreground color is the color you want the brush to be. Then go to Layer>New Fill Layer>Solid Color. Select OK twice. Clip the solid layer to the brush layer. Then drag the brush into your first file.

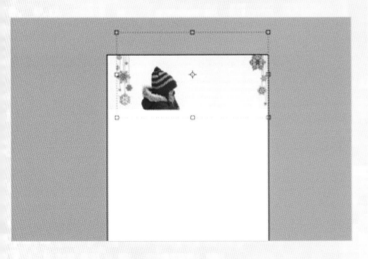

3 Resize the brush until you like how it looks. It's fine if some portions extend off your page. (Note: You can create a brush design with more than one color by duplicating the brush, re-coloring it and erasing portions you don't want to keep. Place the re-colored brush over the original, erasing any duplicated portions.) If you haven't already done so, create the title for your page in a new file, making sure the text layers are merged. Drag the title into the photo file. Once all the elements are arranged to your liking, merge the layers.

Lesson 4:
Adding Text to Photos | Beginner

Audrey Neal

Program:
Microsoft Word

New Technique:
Using text boxes to layer text over a photo

Skills you'll need:
Inserting photos (p. 23)
Adjusting brightness and contrast (p. 23)
Inserting new text boxes (p. 45)
Formatting text boxes (p. 45)
Resizing text boxes (p. 45)
Formatting text (p. 45)
Moving text boxes (p. 47)
Ordering text boxes (p. 49)

I captured these gorgeous photos of my sister in a beautiful outdoor patio in downtown Paducah, Kentucky. Once I started looking at them, I liked how they suggested a sanctuary, a quiet place, which is something my sister had been needing. To create the page, I opened my focal point photo in Word and changed the opacity, adding text boxes to the top and bottom of the photo. I printed the photo on cream-colored cardstock and cut it into five sections. Then I inked the edges of the strips and mounted them on distressed red cardstock before adhering them to the patterned cardstock. I also printed three smaller photos with thin black frames for visual interest, added these to red mats, and placed them on top of the photo strips. I further embellished the page with die-cut pieces, a pearl brad, ribbon and stamps.

DIGITAL SUPPLIES:
AL Worn Machine font (Two Peas in a Bucket); Eight Fifteen font (Internet download)

TRADITIONAL SUPPLIES:
Patterned paper, die cuts (My Mind's Eye); ribbon (Strano); stamps (Purple Onion); chalk ink; brad (unknown); corner rounder; adhesive; pen (Zig)

Although image-editing software can help you create a variety of artistic effects for your pages, Word packs quite a creative punch for a word-processing program. With just a few key techniques, you can create pages to rival any created with complex design programs.

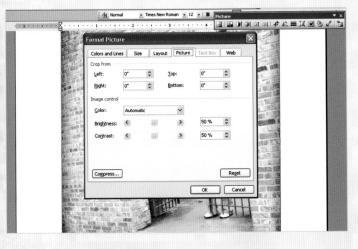

1 Open a new document and insert your focal point photo. To give the photo a dreamy quality, go to the Format Picture menu. Select the Picture tab, then choose Washout from the drop-down menu under Image Control>Color. Adjust the brightness and contrast as needed.

2 Deselect your photo and insert a new text box. Format the text box so it doesn't have a fill or line (so it's transparent). Add additional transparent text boxes, depending on how you want your text to appear on the page. (Note: I created five text boxes: one for the word sanctuary, one for the author, two for separate sections of the quotation, and one for the journaling. It's easier to create overlapping text boxes than to mess with the spacing in one box.)

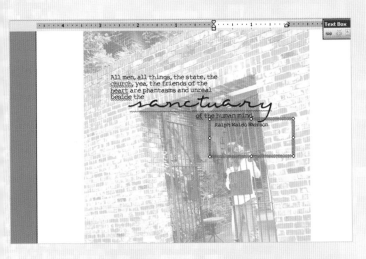

3 Type your text into the various text boxes. Choose different fonts and colors for overlapping boxes to add visual interest. Move your text boxes as desired, changing the order if needed.

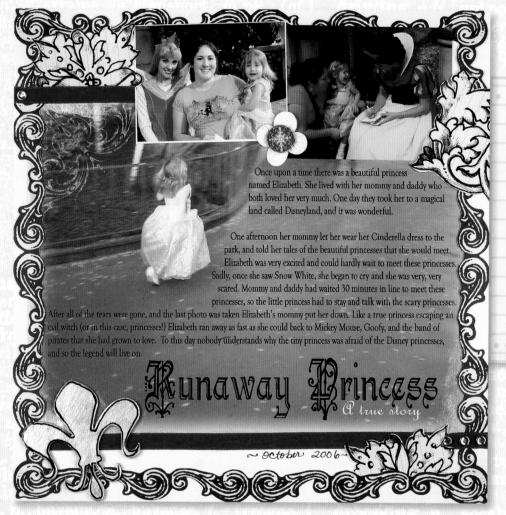

Program:
Adobe Photoshop Elements

New Technique:
Using the Text tool to add text to a photo

Skills you'll need:
Using the Text tool (p. 33)
Moving images (p. 29)
Resizing images (p. 29)
Ordering layers (p. 33, 37)

May Flaum

The meeting of princesses did not go as planned: Our little princess did not like her rendezvous at all! In fact, the moment we put her down, she ran away. When I saw this picture with all the cement, I knew it would be great to journal directly on the photo. To create the page, I sized a photo to approximately 8" x 11" (20cm x 28cm). Then I typed the text and adjusted the page. I printed the page on a sheet of light blue cardstock and edged the paper with a light dusting of metallic paint. I accented the "R" and "P" in the title using a glaze pen. I cut out scroll-edge paper and flowers and adhered the papers, ribbon, photos and other embellishments. Finally, I coated a chipboard accent with a silver metallic paint, then edged it with a black glaze pen.

DIGITAL SUPPLIES:
Grunge overlay by Katie Pertiet (Designer Digitals); decorative photo corner by Dana Zarling (Designer Digitals); French Script and Times New Roman fonts (Microsoft); Kelly Ann Gothic font (Internet download)

TRADITIONAL SUPPLIES:
Cardstock (Prism); patterned paper (Creative Imaginations); ribbon (May Arts); beaded brad (K&Co.); rhinestone brads (Making Memories); flower (Prima); pen (Sakura)

Adding text to a photo in Photoshop Elements allows you to use a photo as a custom background sheet or to create a creative space for journaling.

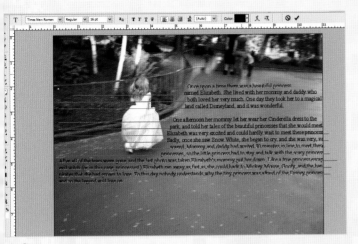

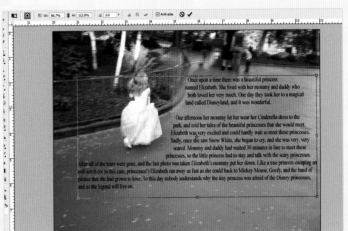

1 Open your photo and adjust the image size to 11" x 8.5" (28cm x 22cm). Select the text tool and choose a font, size and color, and align the text left. Click on the top left of the photo. Hit <enter> to move the starting point for your text down, and hit <tab> to move the starting point to the right. Begin typing your text. At the end of each line hit <enter> to start a new line, using <tab> to move the starting point around portions of the photo.

2 When you're finished typing the text, move and resize the text as needed. At this point, also make any necessary corrections to the text itself. To edit the text, select the text tool, and click in the text where it needs to be fixed.

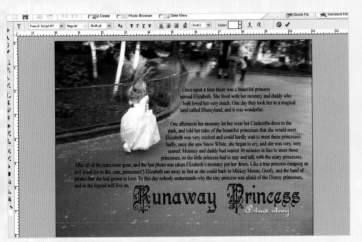

3 To add a title to the photo, select the text tool again, and choose your font style, size and color. Then click on the photo where you want your title to begin and type the title words. Move and resize the title as desired. Repeat this step to add other sections of text to the title.

4 You can give your photo a softer look by adding a grunge overlay. To do so, open the grunge overlay file, and drag it onto your photo. Resize the overlay to fit your photo. Then move the overlay layer behind the text layer. You can add other design elements, such as a decorative corner, by repeating this step.

Lesson 5:
Adding Effects to Text | Beginner

For a long time
she flew

only when she thought
no one else was
watching.

You Are My Everything...

MY LOVE

Audrey Neal

Program:
Adobe Photoshop Elements

New Technique:
Adding texture to text
using the Filter Gallery

Skills you'll need:
Using the Text tool (p. 33)
Selecting layers (p. 35)
Opening the Filter Gallery (p. 29)

My oldest daughter has such a serious, contemplative nature about her. She can be completely goofy, but more often, she seems wise beyond her years. To create a layout that reflected her spirit, I began by printing my text directly onto a piece of patterned paper and mounting it on another paper. Then I attached a photo next to the text. I adhered several torn strips of patterned paper to a background cardstock and placed the photo and text on top of the strips. I added rub-ons to the photo and fitted it with a paper crown and wings, then placed a strip of scalloped paper punched with holes on the page. Last, I added a die-cut heart and rub-on swirl and finished by inking the edges of the page.

DIGITAL SUPPLIES:
2Peas Old Type font (Two Peas in a Bucket)

TRADITIONAL SUPPLIES:
Die-cut shapes, patterned paper, rub-on accents (Fancy Pants); ink; adhesive

Photoshop's Filter Gallery isn't just reserved for adding effects to your photos. Your titles and other text can benefit from the same filter treatments.

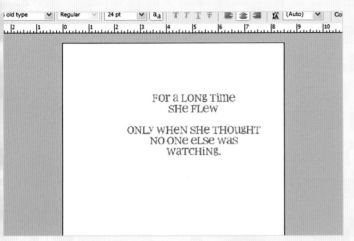

1 Open a blank file, sizing it to the width of the paper onto which you will print the text. Click on the text tool. Choose a thick, hefty font that offers maximum readability, and select a dark color and large size. Type your text, arranging line breaks and spacing as desired. Click on the Simplify button. (See page 95 for an explanation of simplification.)

2 With the text layer selected, open the Filter Gallery. Click on Texture and choose Texturizer. Set the texture to Canvas, scaling to 190, relief to 20 and light direction to bottom. Click OK. The filter may take a few minutes to complete. Additional filters can be added. Also experiment with brushstrokes and other effects. If you don't like the result of a filter, go to Edit>Undo Filter to remove it.

Another Great Idea!

Experiment with other letter filters to achieve different looks for your titles. For example, applying Photoshop's Film Grain filter to the letters in a title creates a look similar to the "Vegas" title on this layout.

DIGITAL SUPPLIES:
Patterned paper from Touch of Funk kit by Kim Christiansen; frame brush from Flowering Horizons kit by Katie Pertiet; digital frame by Rhonna Farrer (Two Peas in a Bucket); digital ABC brushes; Freestyle Script font (Microsoft)

TRADITIONAL SUPPLIES:
Cardstock (Bazzill); patterned paper (American Crafts, KI Memories); star punches; dot accents (Cloud 9); rhinestones (My Minds Eye); pen (Sakura); ink (Ranger)

May Flaum

Lesson 5:
Adding Effects to Text | Intermediate

Program:
Adobe Photoshop Elements

New Technique:
Using brushes to add effects to text

Skills you'll need:
Using the Text tool (p. 33)
Using the Brush tool (p. 35)
Using the Eyedropper tool (p. 35)
Loading brushes (p. 35)
Moving images (p. 29)

May Flaum

Christmas is such a special time of year, and I love capturing the season in my scrapbooks so I can remember Christmas all year long. To create this page, I used Photoshop to make the decorative title, which I then added to the digital photo and designs and printed onto photo paper. I assembled pieces of patterned paper and grosgrain ribbon on a sheet of background cardstock, then added the photo and title. In Word, I typed my journaling over the digital card and printed it out on cardstock. I painted holly chipboard and adhered it to the page along with snowflakes, journaling, a tag and rub-ons.

DIGITAL SUPPLIES:
Frame, tags by Rhonna Farrer (Two Peas in a Bucket); snowflake brush by Katie Pertiet (Designer Digitals)

TRADITIONAL SUPPLIES:
Chipboard accents, patterned paper (BasicGrey, Melissa Frances); Santa rub-on (Daisy D's); paper snowflakes (EK Success); number sticker (BasicGrey); ribbon; paint; corner rounder

As with filters, brushes aren't just for dressing up photos. By adding brushes to text, you can create fancy text and decorative titles to coordinate with any layout theme.

1 Open a new file and also open your photo. In the blank file, select the text tool, choose a font, size and color, and type a word from your title. (Note: Don't forget you can use the eyedropper tool to pick a color from your photo for your text.)

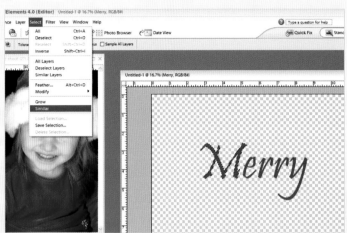

2 Select the Magic Wand tool and click anywhere on the text. Then go to Select>Similar. This selects all the parts in a file that are the same color; in this case, your entire title will be selected. This feature allows you to make changes to the title without affecting the background.

3 Select the Brush tool. Load your brush (if needed), and edit the size, color and opacity of the brush. Then apply the brush to the text until you achieve the desired effect. Repeat this step to add additional brushes to your title.

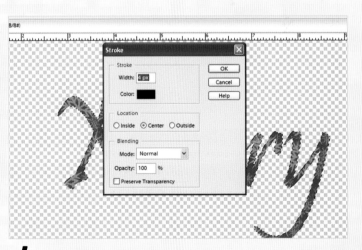

4 To add a stroke (outline) to your title text, go to Edit>Stroke Outline; make sure your title is still selected before you add the stroke outline. In the menu, select the pixel width (I used 4) and color, and click OK. When you're finished go to Select>Deselect to deselect the title. When your title is complete, move it into your photo file.

Part 3 | Paper

We've come to the conclusion that being a scrapbooker means being a paper hoarder. It's just a given—you can't be one without being the other. Of course, that means different things for paper and digital scrapbookers. In fact, most paper scrapbookers cite the tactile nature (even the smell!) of paper as the main reason they don't want to give it up. But that's our point: You don't have to give up anything to incorporate digital techniques into your paper designs.

Paper is one of the most versatile supplies available for scrapbooking. Manufactured in countless patterns, colors and textures, paper has just as many uses: wrinkle it, tear it, stamp it, paint it, ink it, staple it, fold it, crease it—paper can take whatever you dish out. Digital papers offer even more flexibility, since image-editing software gives you the freedom to adjust colors, combine patterns, and more. This chapter leads you through a number of techniques designed to help you maximize the use of digital papers you purchase and provides you with the skills to create your own.

As you make your digital papers, there are a few basics to keep in mind:

- Digital paper files usually are saved as JPEGs and sized at 12″ x 12″ (30cm x 30cm). If you are printing the image as is onto a smaller sheet of paper, be aware that the pattern will retain its original size (12″ [30cm] wide). As a result, the pattern may look too big, and the file may need to be resized before printing.

- Keep the original copy of your paper file intact. If you plan to make alterations, make a copy of the file and work from that.

- Experiment with printing on different paper types. Matte photo paper has a vibrant, smooth look, while cardstock tends to soak up more ink, resulting in more faded colors.

- Do a test print before printing on colored papers as they will affect the color of the final product.

- If printing papers at letter-sized or 12″ x 12″ (30cm x 30cm), set your printer for borderless printing, if possible.

- Once you've printed your digital paper, feel free to distress it the same way you would store-bought paper.

- With digital papers, you can experiment with techniques to create textures prior to printing. Even discerning eyes will have trouble determining whether the texture is digital.

- Remember that you can "cut" your digital paper electronically (by cropping or resizing) rather than printing a full sheet. This preserves printer ink and prevents paper waste.

Lesson 1:
Altering Digital Paper | Beginner

makes me smile, with her
sweet face and silly laugh.
she's a special girl,
no doubt...

Kendall Rebecca

Audrey Neal

Program:
Microsoft Word

New technique:
Adjusting brightness and
contrast of a digital paper

Skills you'll need:
Inserting photos (p. 23)
Adjusting brightness (p. 23)

Every time I look at this picture of my niece, I marvel at how sweet she looks. It's an overwhelming emotion I feel when I see her little face. To create this layout, I adjusted the color scheme of two polka-dot papers. After printing, I trimmed the papers with decorative scissors and mounted them on cardstock. I combined the digital photo with a photo mask and decorative text, then printed it and rounded the corners before adding it to the layout. I cut out the circle pattern from another sheet of paper and adhered that to the page, overlapping my photo. I finished by adding journaling strips, a title, and flower and rhinestone accents.

DIGITAL SUPPLIES:
Patterned papers, photo masks and decorative text from Bloom kit by Tracy Ann Robinson

TRADITIONAL SUPPLIES:
Cardstock (Bazzill); chipboard letters, rhinestones (Heidi Swapp); flower ribbon (Making Memories); brads; decorative scissors; corner rounder; adhesive (Beacon); pen (Sakura)

What do you do if you really like a set of digital papers, but the colors are too bold for your layout? Tone them down! One of the advantages of printing your own papers is being able to modify the colors to suit your needs.

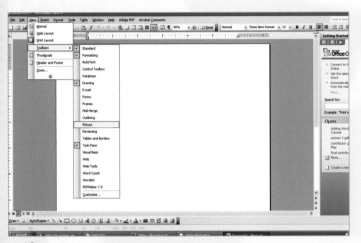

1 Open a new document and open the Picture toolbar. Insert your digital paper as you would a photo; go to Insert>Picture>From File. Navigate to the proper folder and select your paper.

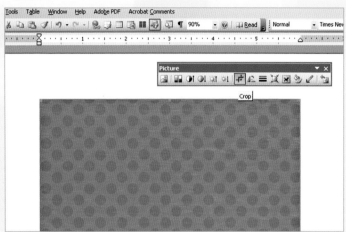

2 Resize the paper as needed. To make the pattern smaller in proportion to a smaller image size, use the handles to resize it. To maintain the pattern's size as the paper gets smaller, crop the image. Click on the Crop icon in the Picture toolbar and drag your mouse from any of the corners. (I cropped my image to 8″ x 4″ [20cm x 10cm].)

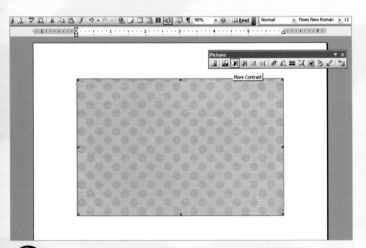

3 To lighten your paper, increase the brightness. (I clicked four times.) If you want to bring out the pattern detail, increase the constrast as desired. (I clicked two times.)

4 At this point, your paper is complete. You can insert a second paper into the document and repeat the process. (I cropped my second image to measure 8″ x 6″ [20cm x 15cm].)

Lesson 1:
Altering Digital Paper | Intermediate

May Flaum

Program:
Adobe Photoshop Elements

New technique:
Adding decorative overlays
to a digital paper

Skills you'll need:
Moving images (p. 29)
Resizing images (p. 51)

I chose a soft color palette for this page to allow the photos to really stand out. I wanted to capture my daughter at this precious age and preserve her sweet and sassy nature. By using overlays on an ordinary polka-dot paper, I was able to make a one-of-a-kind background that coordinates with the frame I used on the focal point photo. To create this page, I added a digital frame to both the background paper and the focal point photo. I printed the digital paper on cream, rather than white cardstock, to produce a soft, aged look. Then I adhered the three photos to the background page, along with a journaling tag, letters and the chipboard heart. I also attached the fabric flower and arrow, rub-ons, word embellishment and my journaling. Finally, I printed the number 2 on fabric paper, cut it out, and placed it on top of the flower to complete the page.

DIGITAL SUPPLIES:
Brush, frame, grunge overlay, patterned papers by Katie Pertiet (Designer Digitals)

TRADITIONAL SUPPLIES:
Cardstock (Prism); cotton paper (Jacquard); epoxy, journal accent, letter stickers by Karen Russell (Creative Imaginations); chipboard heart (Melissa Frances); fabric flower (Junkitz); arrow (Scenic Route); rub-on accents (BasicGrey); pen (Sakura)

Not only is adding overlays to digital papers simple, but it also allows you to create custom looks suited to each individual project.

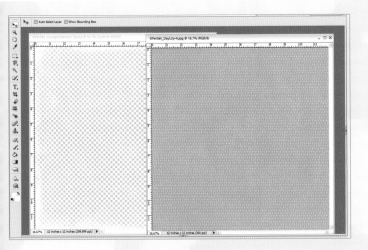

1 Open the digital paper and any overlays you want to work with. You can use as many overlays as you like for this lesson. You can also add brushes and frames in addition to or in place of an overlay, following the same steps. (I used a grunge overlay and a decorative overlay.)

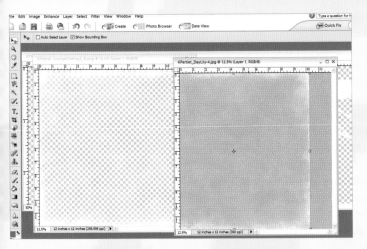

2 Position the grunge overlay first. Drag the grunge overlay into the digital paper file, and place the overlay over the paper, resizing it as needed. To include the edges of the overlay when the paper is printed, resize the overlay to the same size as the paper you will be printing (e.g., make the overlay 8.5″ x 11″ [22cm x 28cm] if your paper will be printed at that size.)

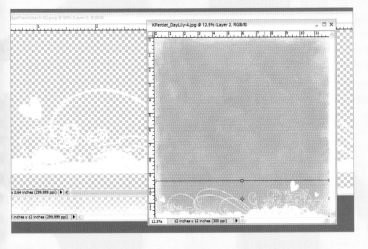

3 Next, drag additional overlays into the digital paper file. Again, resize them to fit your paper. Once you're satisfied with the look of the paper, you're ready to print!

Lesson 2:
Mixing Digital Papers | Beginner

Program:
Adobe Photoshop Elements

New technique:
Using the Marquee tool to create a striped digital paper

Skills you'll need:
Moving images (p. 29)
Using the Marquee tool (p. 33)
Merging all layers (p. 33)

May Flaum

With just a click of my camera, I can preserve beauty and keep flowers forever. Almost as simply, I can create custom patterned paper for my layouts. To create this layout, I began by merging different papers into one file, creating a striped paper to use as the background for a page. I printed the stripes on a sheet of cream-colored cardstock. I then tore the bottom of a coordinating piece of patterned paper and inked all the edges. I adhered the paper to the center of the page and layered my photo over the paper. I attached the title and tab and added journaling and rub-ons. I placed a piece of ribbon down the right side to complete the page.

DIGITAL SUPPLIES:
Patterned papers from Flowering Horizons Kit by Katie Pertiet and from Welcome Home kit by Lynn Grieveson

TRADITIONAL SUPPLIES:
Cardstock (Prism); patterned paper (K&Co.); letter stickers (Heidi Grace); rub-on accents (BasicGrey);
tab (Creative Imaginations); ribbon (unknown); ink (Ranger); pen (Sakura)

Mixing strips of patterned paper allows you to create your own sophisticated pattern while providing a way to incorporate all of your favorite digital papers into one design.

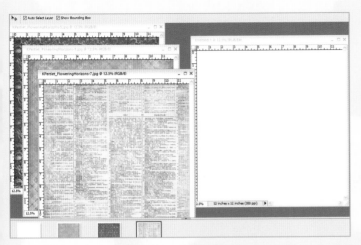

1 Open the digital papers you want to use, and then open a blank file. (Note: Coordinating stripes is easy if you use the papers included in one digital kit.)

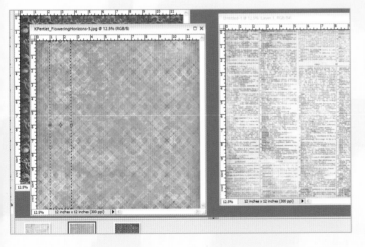

2 Move one of the patterned papers into the blank file. In a different digital paper file, use the Marquee tool to select a rectangular strip of the paper. Drag the selected area onto the new file (with the first patterned paper).

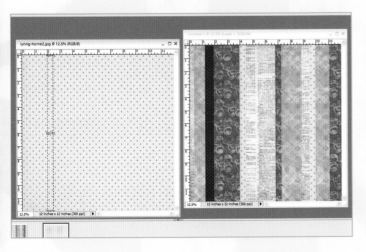

3 Continue using the Marquee and Move tools to insert strips of paper, in varying widths, into the new file. If you want to include multiple strips of the same paper, simply copy (<ctrl+C>) and paste (<ctrl+P>) the layer with that strip. You can then resize the strip, but its pattern will be distorted. (Note: If you want varying widths of the same paper without distortion you need to drag two different selections into the new file.) After all the strips are in place, merge the layers.

Mixing Digital Papers|Intermediate

Program:
Adobe Photoshop Elements

New technique:
Using the Eraser tool to combine digital papers

Skills you'll need:
Resizing images (p. 29)
Moving images (p. 29)
Erasing images (p. 35)

May Flaum

Searching for subject inspiration, I found myself looking at a statue I have on the wall and thinking about my late uncle. I realized I should scrap the statue so its meaning would never be lost. To create this layout, I scanned the small photo I keep with the statue and placed it in a new Photoshop file. I opened the digital flower rub-on and frame and placed those in the file with the photo. I printed two copies of the image on plain white cardstock. I cut the whole image out of one sheet and cut just the photo out of the other sheet, and then attached the two pieces. In Word, I typed the text for journaling and printed it to test its location on the page. Then I taped the label to the sheet of paper (over the journaling) and printed it out again; this time with the journaling printed on the label. I assembled the label along with photos, a chipboard title, ribbon and other elements. I stamped decorative accents on the page and finished by edging the background paper with a gold leafing pen and inkpad.

DIGITAL SUPPLIES:
Patterned paper by Lynn Grieveson (Designer Digitals); blue flowers, frame by Katie Pertiet (Designer Digitals)

TRADITIONAL SUPPLIES:
Cardstock (Prism); chipboard letters (K&Co.); chipboard circle (Imagination Project); chipboard photo corner (Scenic Route); flower (Heidi Grace); stamps (Sugarloaf); ink (Ranger); gold leafing pen (Krylon); pen (Fiskars)

Combining two patterns is a fun technique with which to experiment. Using the eraser tool on one paper to make another shine through always results in a sweet surprise.

1 Open the two patterned papers you want to use for this project and also open a blank file. (This technique works best with patterns that are very different, such as a simple dot and more detailed flower pattern.) Edit and resize the two papers as needed.

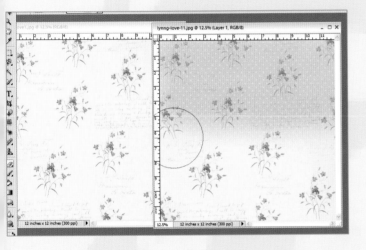

2 Drag the pattern that will be on the bottom into the blank file, then drag the other one on top. Keep in mind that the paper on top is the one you'll erase, and the paper on the bottom is the one that will show through. (I put my flowered paper on top and erased it to reveal the dots.) Select the Eraser tool, adjust the eraser's opacity and choose the size as desired. Then erase the top paper using one continuous brush stroke. (Note: Erasing in more than one stroke will produce an uneven look.)

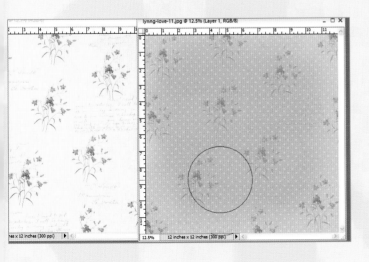

3 You can adjust the opacity further and make another continuous sweep with the eraser. Continue erasing the top page until you achieve the desired effect.

things change...

i admit, sometimes i look in the mirror and have trouble recognizing the woman looking back at me. the concept of myself that i carry around inside my head doesn't match up to these faces. proof that change happens.

talkin bout an evolution

Audrey Neal

Program:
Adobe Photoshop Elements

New technique:
Adding a gradient fill to a digital brush

Skills you'll need:
Using the Brush tool (p. 35)
Resizing images (p. 29)
Moving images (p. 29)
Clipping layers (p. 37)
Merging all layers (p. 33)

Scrolling through some photos, I came across three headshots of myself. I was struck by how much I've changed over the past three years. To create this layout, I printed the flowery graphic brush on white cardstock. I attached the flowers with brads and added rhinestones, a rub-on and a chipboard title. I printed the three photos and the frames onto a transparency, then cut them out and glued them to the layout, adding more brads and rhinestones. I mounted the entire layout on black cardstock and added some rub-on lines for my journaling.

DIGITAL SUPPLIES:
Brushes and frames by Michelle Coleman (Little Dreamer Designs)

TRADITIONAL SUPPLIES:
Cardstock (Paper Studio); chipboard letters (Heidi Swapp); rub-on letters (Imagination Project); rub-on accents (Hambly); flowers (Doodlebug, Prima); brads; rhinestones (My Mind's Eye); transparency; adhesive (Beacon); pen (Sakura)

Designing your own patterned paper doesn't have to be a dream. With Photoshop Elements and digital brushes, you can create designs galore.

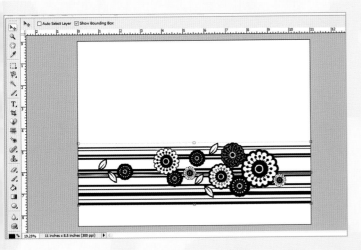

1 Open a blank 11″ x 8″ (28cm x 20cm) file. Choose a brush from the Brush toolbar and stamp it on your page. Resize and adjust the position of the brush.

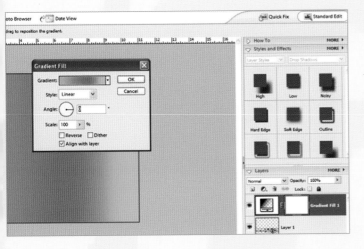

2 To achieve a multi-tonal look for your design, select Layer>New Fill Layer>Gradient. Choose the gradient you want your design to have. Then click on the drop-down arrow to select your gradient color. Change the angle to zero degrees. Click OK when you're finished.

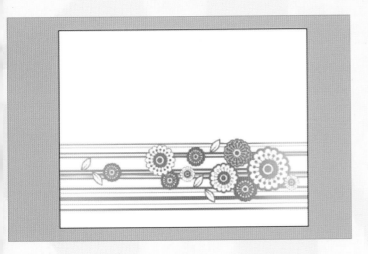

3 Clip the gradient layer to the brush layer to make your brush colored. Then merge the layers when finished.

Lesson 3:
Using Brushes and Filters | Intermediate

6-3B

REaP

Your mind
is a garden
your thoughts are
the harvest
can be either
flowers or weeds
(unknown)

You only get out of Life what you put
into it. Luck has nothing to do with it,
although it may seem so at times. If there
is nothing else I can pass on to You from Your
poppa, at least there is this. Hard work and
initiative do pay off in the Long Run. Theyde

Program:
Adobe Photoshop
Elements

New technique:
Using filters to add
texture to digital paper

Skills you'll need:
Opening the Filter Gallery (p. 29)
Merging all layers (p. 33)

Audrey Neal

My dad really pushed me to succeed in college. He worked at middle-class jobs that involved hard labor his whole life, and like most parents, he wanted more for me. It wasn't until I graduated that I really learned how much hard work can impact a person's life. It's a lesson I want to make sure my daughters learn. To create this layout, I ran filters on two digital papers. I printed them, inked the edges, and adhered them to the background cardstock. To create the focal point photo, I added a digital quote, then printed. I added the other two photos to the layout, then placed the focal point photo and journaling mat over those. To finish, I added the chipboard title and layers of fabric flowers, which I created digitally and printed onto fabric.

DIGITAL SUPPLIES:
Flowers, papers, decorative text by Mindy Terasawa (Designer Digitals)

TRADITIONAL SUPPLIES:
Cardstock (Bazzill); patterned paper (Mustard Moon); chipboard letters (Heidi Swapp); brad; ink (Clearsnap); adhesive (Beacon); pen (Sakura)

Although digital papers print flat, you can fake tons of texture using Photoshop's filters.

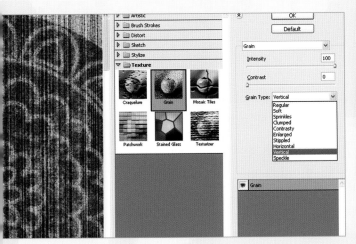

1 Open one of the papers you want to use for this project. To create the textured weave effect (shown on my floral paper) begin by opening the Filter Gallery and going to Texture>Grain. Use the following settings: intensity—100; contrast—0; and grain type—vertical. Then select New Effect Layer. Once the filter has run, repeat this step but change grain type to horizontal.

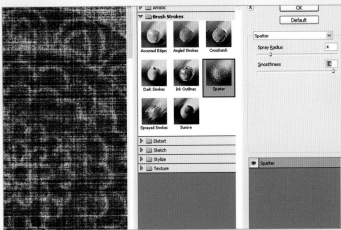

2 Next, select Brush Strokes>Spatter. Set the spray radius to 4 and the smoothness to 14. Select OK to run the filter.

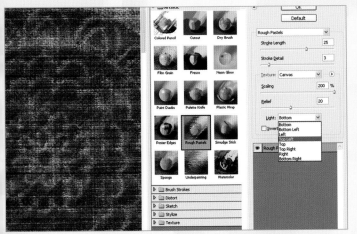

3 Then run another filter, this time choosing Artistic>Rough Pastels. Use the following settings: stroke length—25; stroke detail—3; texture—canvas; scaling—200; relief—20; and light—top left. Select OK. Merge the layers.

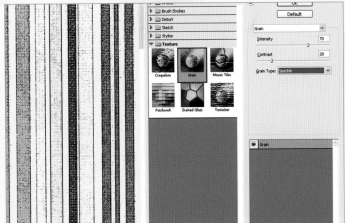

4 To add texture to another paper (such as on my striped paper), select Texture>Grain. Set Intensity to 70, Contrast to 20 and select Speckle as the grain type. Also run the Rough Pastels filter (see step 3), then merge the layers.

Note: Although this lesson walks you through using filters with specific settings to achieve a certain look, you should experiment with the different filters and settings on your digital papers. Each filter offers a different result, and filters can be used in various combinations and settings to create numerous looks.

Lesson 4:
Creating Paper with Text and Shapes
Beginner

He is a

fUN·gUY

i play!

that C·man

smile

Connor loved being able to get on the inflatable playground at the 4th of July celebration in Bartlett. He bounced, rolled, flopped and fell— and the laughs didn't stop the entire time. He was so proud of himself and all he could do!

Audrey Neal

Program:
Microsoft Word

New technique:
Using AutoShapes to create a patterned paper

Skills you'll need:
Adusting page orientation (p. 23)

My nephew Connor was nothing but giggles on a bouncy playground set up for a 4th of July celebration. We all stood and watched him for the longest time, loving how much he was enjoying himself. To make this layout, I created the background pattern in Word and printed two copies. I trimmed those, rounded one corner on each and mounted them on black cardstock. I added a graph-patterned paper and journaling, along with a thin orange strip with curved edges. I added a digital frame to the photos and then printed and attached them to the layout. I finished by adding arrows punched from orange cardstock and the green background pattern, as well as chipboard and plastic letters, printed words, stickers and brads for embellishment.

DIGITAL SUPPLIES:
Schmootzy frame by Nancie Rowe Janitz (ScrapArtist)

TRADITIONAL SUPPLIES:
Cardstock (Stampin' Up); patterned paper (Scenic Route); chipboard and plastic letters (Heidi Swapp); letter stickers (Making Memories); epoxy stickers (Me & My Big Ideas, Provo Craft); brads; arrow punch (Fiskars); corner rounder; adhesive (Beacon); pen (Sakura)

Sometimes the most basic shapes can create lively patterned papers, especially when used in bright color combinations. Using Word's AutoShapes makes creating a polka-dot pattern a snap.

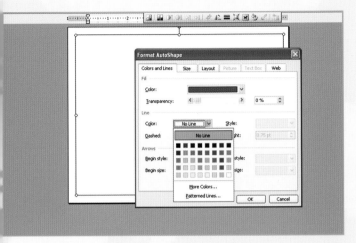

1 Open a new document and change the page orientation to landscape. Open the Drawing toolbar by going to View>Toolbars>Drawing. Select the rectangle icon from the toolbar and draw a square that fills up your entire page. Right-click on the square and select Format AutoShape. Choose No Line and set the fill color to your desired choice. (I chose green.)

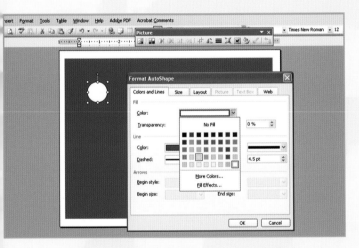

2 Select the oval shape from your Drawing toolbar and click on your screen. Use the corner handles to adjust the size of your circle; press <shift> while resizing to maintain a circular shape. Then go back to the Format AutoShape menu. Choose a thick line weight (I used 4.5) and change the line color, then set a fill color for your circle.

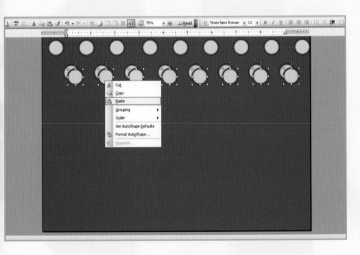

3 To repeat the circles in a polka-dot pattern across the page, simply copy and paste. Start by moving the original circle to the top left corner of the screen (by clicking on the circle and dragging your mouse). Select the circle and go to Edit>Copy and Edit>Paste. Continue to copy and paste to create a row of circles. Then click on all the circles at once, copy and paste them, and move the new row of circles underneath the first, staggering the two rows. Continue copying and pasting rows down the page.

Lesson 4:
Creating Paper with Text and Shapes
Intermediate

May Flaum

Program:
Microsoft Word

New technique:
Creating patterned paper using text and WordArt

Skills you'll need:
Adjusting page orientation (p. 23)
Formatting text (p. 45)
Inserting WordArt (p. 47)
Formatting WordArt (p. 53)
Moving WordArt (p. 53)

These photos remind me of all the fun my daughter and I have in the garden together; the thought makes me smile. Often I get caught up in daily life and forget to take snapshots. One of my goals this year was to capture more details like this. To create the page, I began by printing the text "pattern" on cardstock. I used pinking shears on the top and bottom edges and adhered the paper to the cardstock background. Then I typed my journaling in Word and used WordArt to add the colorful title. I printed my journaling on Kraft cardstock and cut it out, then adhered it to the page along with the photos. I stamped the flowers onto cream cardstock and colored them with glaze pens. After allowing it to dry, I attached the stamp to the layout, along with flowers, rub-ons, brads and other accents. Finally, I added flourish stamps and painted the edges of the layout.

DIGITAL SUPPLIES:
Beef Broccoli, Fabulous and Tokyo Girl fonts (Two Peas in a Bucket); Freestyle Script font (Microsoft); Gardener font by Tia Bennett (Autumn Leaves)

TRADITIONAL SUPPLIES:
Cardstock (Prism); chipboard accents (Scenic Route); flowers (Heidi Swapp, Prima); photo corner (American Crafts); brads; rub-on accents (Cloud 9); stamps (Autumn Leaves); paint, ink (Ranger); pen (Sakura)

Adding a few lines of colored text to create custom paper adds a personal touch and sets the perfect tone for a page.

1 Open a new document and set the page orientation to landscape. Choose a font for your first line of text. Starting at the top of the page, type a line of text, repeating a word or adding a sentence until the text reaches the right side of the page. Change the font and then begin typing your second line of text. Create 3 to 5 more rows of text.

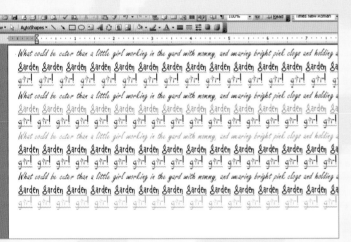

2 Make sure each line runs the width of the page. Copy and paste your lines of text so they repeat down the page. When the page is full, highlight lines at random and change the font color as desired.

3 Use WordArt to add flowers and other images to the rows of text. Go to the WordArt gallery and choose the style. Then change the font to a dingbat font (such as Webdings). You may need to type various keys until the image you want appears (e.g., typing a "J" creates a happy face). Resize and color the WordArt images as needed, and move them to different locations on the page.

Lesson 5:
Altering Photos | Beginner/Intermediate

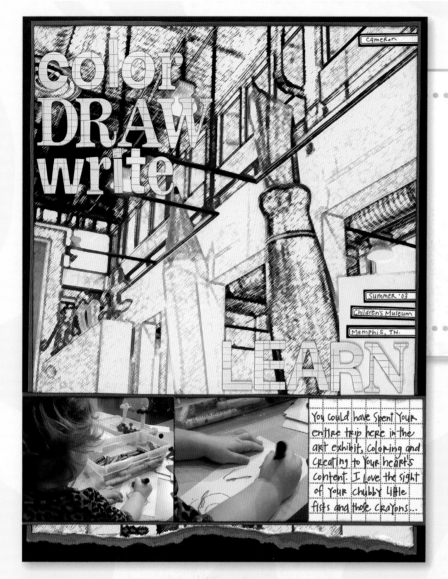

Program:
Adobe Photoshop Elements

New technique:
Creating background paper by
applying filters to photos

Skills you'll need:
Moving photos (p. 29)
Opening the Filter Gallery (p. 29)

Audrey Neal

When I'm out with the girls, I love to get background shots, in addition to photos of them actually doing something. Museums, zoos, parks—it doesn't matter. I just like having a means of remembering our location, as well as what we did. Background photos work wonderfully on pages after applying a digital filter. To create this layout, I applied a filter to my photo and printed it as an 8″ x 10″ (20cm x 25cm) sheet. I tore the bottom edge of the photo, then matted it on purple cardstock and tore that paper's edge as well. Then I matted them both on black cardstock. I printed two more wallet-sized photos and mounted them on purple cardstock. I then inked all the edges. I added graph paper and journaling to the page, along with chipboard letters and small stickers for additional detail.

DIGITAL SUPPLIES:
None

TRADITIONAL SUPPLIES:
Cardstock (Stampin' Up); patterned paper (Scenic Route); chipboard letters (Heidi Swapp); sticker accents (7gypsies);
ink (Clearsnap); adhesive (Beacon); pen (Sakura)

Using a large photograph as a background is a common technique among graphic designers. Adding a filter to a photo, mimicking this technique on your layout, will give your page a look that's both modern and creative.

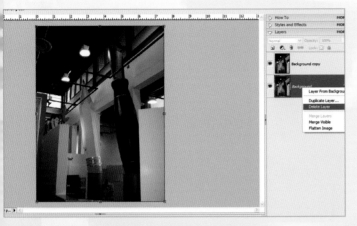

1 Open your photo and a new file. Drag a copy of the photo to the new file, and close the original. Make any necessary adjustments to your image. (I adjusted the brightness of my image to 75 and the contrast to 20.)

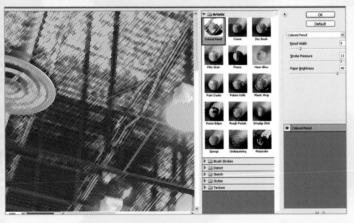

2 Open the Filter Gallery and go to Artistic>Colored Pencil. Select the following settings: pencil width—5; stroke pressure—13; paper brightness—40. Click OK to run the filter. Make any other adjustments to the photo as needed before printing.

Another Great Idea!

Play around with Photoshop's filters to create different looks for your photo page backgrounds. The angle brush filter will produce the effect shown on this page. You can create the checkerboard pattern using the cookie cutter tool. Merge the layers when you're finished using the cookie cutter tool, and then apply the filter.

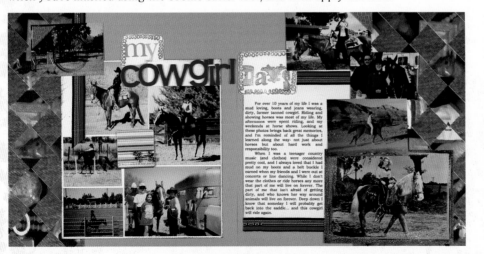

DIGITAL SUPPLIES:
Bookman Old Style font (Microsoft)

TRADITIONAL SUPPLIES:
Cardstock; chipboard letters, photo corners (Scenic Route); chipboard square, letter stickers (Heidi Grace); ribbon (Strano); stamps (Fiskars, Fontwerks, Technique Tuesday); rub-on accent (Luxe Designs); embossing enamel, ink (Ranger); greeting card (unknown)

May Flaum

Lesson 5:
Altering Photos | Advanced

May Flaum

Program:
Adobe Photoshop
Elements

New technique:
Creating background paper
by adding overlays, brushes
and filters to photos

Skills you'll need:
Moving images (p. 29)
Resizing images (p. 29)
Using the Brush tool (p. 35)
Opening the Filter Gallery (p. 29)
Merging all layers (p. 33)

I harbor a love for buttons; in fact, it runs in the family. I love that I'm following in the crafty footsteps of my mom
and grandma, so I just had to dedicate a page to our shared obsession. To create the layout, I first printed the button
background and the focal point photo (after adding digital elements to both). I attached a cardstock mat to the
photo, then attached that and the button background to a sheet of pink patterned paper. I cut a journaling block
in half, then reattached the pieces to create a tall box. I added journaling, a tab and letter stickers to the page, then
outlined the title in pen. To complete the layout, I stamped onto Kraft cardstock, added more journaling and adhered it to the page along with buttons and lace.

DIGITAL SUPPLIES:
Brush, grunge overlay by Katie Pertiet (Designer Digitals); frame by Rhonna Farrer (Two Peas in a Bucket);
journal block from Sweet Baby Chic kit by Michelle Coleman

TRADITIONAL SUPPLIES:
Cardstock (Prism); patterned paper (Mustard Moon); letter stickers (Heidi Grace, Making Memories); buttons (Autumn Leaves, Melissa Frances);
stamp (Fontwerks); fabric tab (Scrapworks); lace, metal embellishments (unknown); pen (Sakura)

Overlays and brushes provide another great way to alter your photos for use as backgrounds. And taking a cue from your layout's topic to choose a background for the page ensures a well-coordinated look.

1 Open the photo you're using for the project and resize it as needed to fit your layout. Also open a grunge overlay. Move the overlay into the photo file, rotate (Image>Rotate) and resize it to fit over the photo.

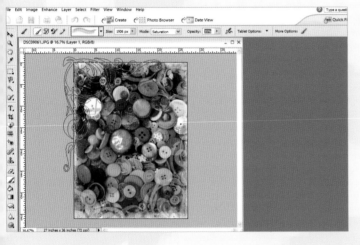

2 Next, add a decorative brush to the photo. Adjust the brush's mode and opacity (I set the mode to Saturation and opacity to 35 percent) so the brush work will just lighten the stamped area. Stamp your brush over the edges of the photo.

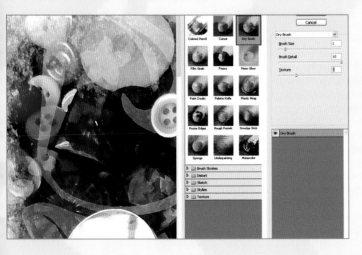

3 Finish the photo's stylized look by adding an artistic filter. Choose Dry Brush from the Artistic menu in the Filter Gallery, and adjust the brush size and detail until you're satisfied with the effect. (I set the brush size, brush detail, and texture to 1, 10 and 2, respectively.) Merge your layers to finish.

Part 4 | Embellishments

The name says it all. Embellishments add texture and personality, making even a simple design pop. The digital realm offers electronic versions of embellishments you already know and love—like brads, flowers, and ribbons. Plus it provides tools to create your own embellishments.

In this chapter, we look at various ways to use and create embellishments in Word and Photoshop Elements. Some of the topics include altering the color of pre-made embellishments, making your own brushes and putting multiple elements together to create a digital layout.

Before we get started with the lessons, here are a few points to remember about digital embellishments:

- The digital kits included with this book are bursting with embellishments. They can be resized and re-colored to fit your specific projects.

- When you find yourself with unused space on a piece of paper, think about printing a few extra embellishments. I (May) save all of my extra printouts in a box and then cut them out while watching TV.

- Micro-tip scissors (like those from Fiskars) are a hand-saver when cutting out embellishments.

- Using embellishments straight from the printer is a great addition to a page. But you can add your own pen work, glitter, dimensional adhesive and other accents to personalize your embellishments even more.

- Consider what type of paper you're printing on when creating embellishments. Vellum, transparencies and other specialty papers will add a different look and feel to your projects. For example, textured cardstock adds a nice matte finish while glossy photo paper produces embellishments with sheen.

Audrey Neal

Program:
Microsoft Word

New technique:
Inserting digital embellishments
into a document for printing

Skills you'll need:
Inserting images (p. 23)
Cropping images (p. 67)
Resizing images (p. 27)

When I saw the decorative text from the Authentic Me kit,
I immediately knew I needed to combine it with a photo of
my sister. The words said just what I needed her to hear.
To create this layout, I digitally combined the decorative
text and photo frame with my photo then printed it. I
printed other embellishments and inked their edges. I
layered two pieces of inked cardstock, one with a large
ripped edge, and added my printed elements. I added
journaling to the notebook paper and finished by adding
ribbons, staples and buttons.

DIGITAL SUPPLIES:
Frame, heart, labels, notebook paper and decorative text from Authentic Me
kit by Lauren Reid

TRADITIONAL SUPPLIES:
Cardstock (Bazzill); buttons (Autumn Leaves); ribbon (Strano);
ink (Clearsnap); adhesives (3M, Beacon); staples; pen (Sakura)

The simplest way to use digital embellishments is to print them as they are. Save time and paper by inserting your paper and all your embellishments into one Word document.

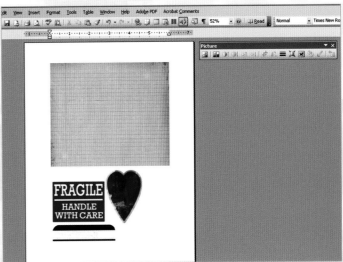

1 Open a new document and insert your digital paper file. Make sure the Picture toolbar is open and use it to crop your paper. Crop or resize the paper to fit your layout.

2 Insert coordinating embellishments one at a time as you would insert photos (Insert>Picture>From File). Leave space around each element if you want them to have a white border. Resize the elements as desired before printing.

Another Great Idea!

Here's another example of how to use printed digital elements. To re-create this look, simply insert a star and digital candles into a blank Word document, print the embellishments on white cardstock and cut. Simple!

DIGITAL SUPPLIES:
Birthday Bash Digital kit by Dani Mogstad (Design By Dani)

TRADITIONAL SUPPLIES:
Cardstock (Die Cuts With A View); chipboard letters (Heidi Swapp); metal clip (Making Memories); ribbon (unknown); corner rounder; decorative scissors; adhesive (Beacon, Therm O Web); pen (Zig)

Audrey Neal

Lesson 1:
Using Digital Embellishments
Intermediate

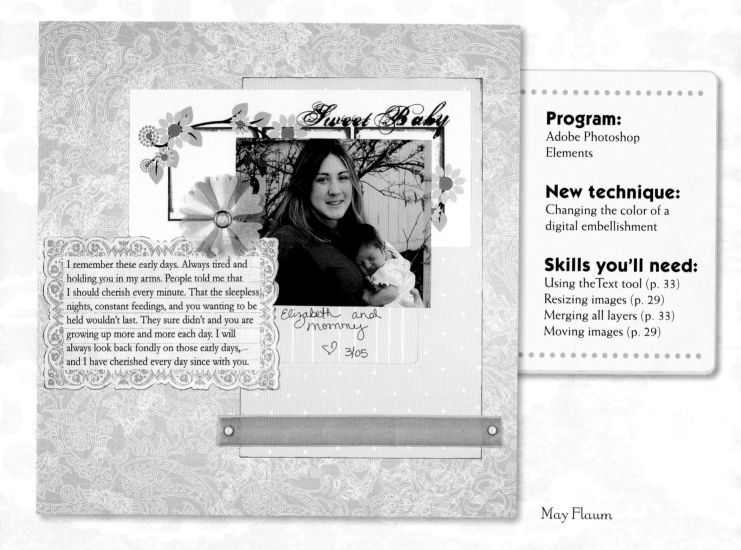

Program:
Adobe Photoshop
Elements

New technique:
Changing the color of a
digital embellishment

Skills you'll need:
Using the Text tool (p. 33)
Resizing images (p. 29)
Merging all layers (p. 33)
Moving images (p. 29)

May Flaum

I have very few photos of those first few weeks of motherhood, and those that I do have I cherish. By re-coloring the embellishment from the Sweet Baby Chic kit, I was able to make it work for my sweet and simple page. To create this layout, I printed the title and flower embellishment on white cardstock and adhered it to background paper along with a piece of polka-dot patterned paper (with inked edges). Then I attached the photo, ribbon and tag. I printed a journaling block with text, inked the edges, and attached it to the page. Finally, I added tissue flowers and brads.

DIGITAL SUPPLIES:
Sweet Baby Chic kit by Michelle Coleman

TRADITIONAL SUPPLIES:
Patterned paper (Luxe Designs); brads, ribbon (Making Memories); flowers (Prima); ink (Ranger); pen (Sakura)

Altering the colors of digital embellishments can help you make every element work for your projects and get more use out of what you have in your collection.

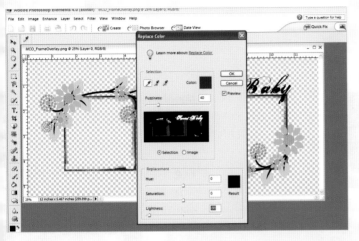

1 Open your embellishment (as you would a picture file) and go to the Replace Color menu (Enhance>Color>Replace Color). Click on the color in the embellishment that you want to change. Then adjust the hue, saturation and lightness of the color until you achieve the desired shade. Repeat this step with any other colors you want to edit.

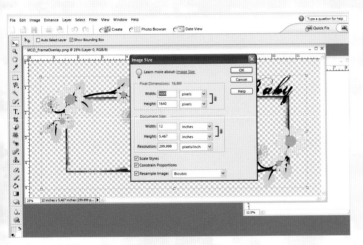

2 You can use the Image Size menu to resize the embellishment to fit your layout. To change the size, right-click on the top of the file, choose Image Size, and adjust as needed. Then move the image into a blank 8.5" x 11" (22cm x 28cm) file.

3 Open your journaling embellishment and follow the steps above to re-color, if needed. Then use the text tool to type your journaling. Resize as needed and merge your layers. Drag the journaling block onto the letter-sized page.

Note: If you're working with an embellishment or paper that's monochromatic, you can change the color of the entire image by going to Enhance>Color>Hue/Saturation.

Program:
Adobe Photoshop
Elements

New technique:
Making a custom brush
embellishment using a
scanned drawing

Skills you'll need:
Using the Magic Wand
tool (p. 63)
Using the Brush tool (p. 35)
Using the Eyedropper tool (p. 51)

Audrey Neal

When my little girls were born, I swore I'd never dress them in pink. Unfortunately, both of them looked completely adorable in pink, so I ended up eating my words. My friend's little girl is another vision in pink, which was the guiding color for this layout. To create the page, I layered scalloped cardstock over a solid square, then punched holes along the scalloped edges. I printed the heart doodles in pink, then cut them out and framed them with chipboard (covered with digital patterned paper). I tied the frames together with floral ribbon and layered them over my three photos and journaling. Brads, velvet words, chipboard and cardstock trim add an extra feminine touch to the page.

Photos by: Amy Martin

DIGITAL SUPPLIES:
Paper from Sweet Baby Chic kit by Michelle Coleman 💿

TRADITIONAL SUPPLIES:
Cardstock (Bazzill); scalloped cardstock (Doodlebug); word stickers (Making Memories); chipboard accents (BasicGrey, Deluxe Designs, Junkitz); journaling accent (Heidi Swapp); hole punch; brads (Bazzill, Paper Studio); ribbon (unknown); adhesive (Beacon); pen (Sakura)

You can turn your own doodles into a set of brushes that can be used as embellishments and re-colored and resized with just a few clicks of your mouse.

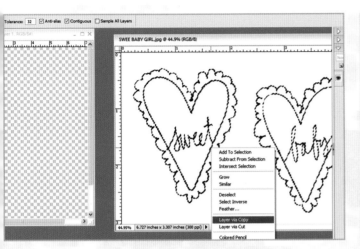

1 Begin by drawing an image on a sheet of white paper with a black marker or fine-tipped pen. Scan the image and save it as a JPEG, then open the file. Also open a blank file (bigger than your drawing). Select the Magic Wand tool, then click on your drawing to select it. Right-click and select Layer Via Copy.

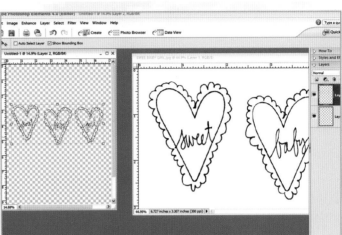

2 Drag the new layer into the blank file. Go to Edit>Define Brush. Create a name for your brush and click OK. Close all open files.

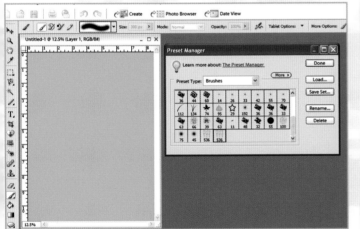

3 Open a new letter-sized file. Select a background color. Use the Paint Bucket tool to fill the background layer with the color of your choice. Click on the Brush tool and select a new color for your brush. Click on the Fly-out menu and choose Preset Manager. Scroll down to select your brush, then choose Save Set. Name your brush and click OK. Click Done to exit.

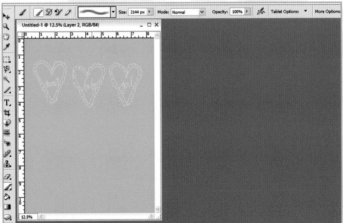

4 Open a new layer and click on the screen to apply your brush. To re-color your brush, set your foreground color with the Eyedropper tool and select Layer>New Fill Layer>Solid Color. Click OK twice, then merge the layers.

Lesson 2:
Making Brushes | Advanced

The work that has been done on the houses in Lowertown is just incredible.

The entire neighborhood is undergoing the same kind of renovation. It's some great eye candy.

christmas in Paducah's lowertown

Audrey Neal

Program:
Adobe Photoshop
Elements

New technique:
Creating a brush embellishment
using custom shapes

Skills you'll need:
Moving images (p. 29)
Merging all layers (p. 33)
Opening new layers (p. 37)
Using the Brush tool (p. 35)

What's not to love about a giant giraffe statue at Christmastime? The artists in Paducah's Lowertown district have some incredible ideas for holiday decorating, which I was lucky enough to capture on film. To begin creating this layout, I opened a polka-dot digital paper. I digitally added a black stroke, followed by a white stroke to the focal point photo, then added black strokes to three smaller photos and placed them behind the main photo. After printing the photos, I printed a holly brush on the top and bottom of the green cardstock, as well as on a strip of canvas paper. I mounted the photos on the cardstock, along with printed journaling tags. I attached the canvas strip, embellished with brads, and finished with a title made of chipboard and rub-ons.

DIGITAL SUPPLIES:
Dot paper, tags from Welcome Home kit
by Lynn Grieveson 🖭

TRADITIONAL SUPPLIES:
Cardstock (Bazzill); canvas paper (Office Depot); chipboard letters (Heidi Swapp); rub-on letters
(American Crafts); brads (Paper Studio); corner rounder; adhesive (Beacon); pen (Sakura)

The shapes in Photoshop's custom shape tool inventory don't have to be used alone. Combine a series of shapes to create a custom brush embellishment for your layout.

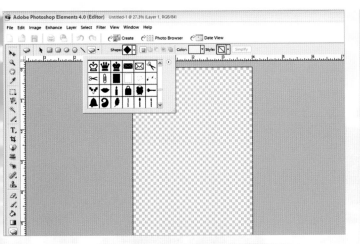

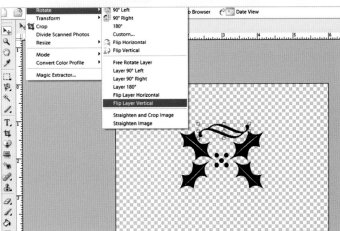

1 Open a new blank file, about 4" x 6" (10cm x 15cm). Click on the Custom Shape tool. Select the drop-down arrow in the Custom Shape toolbar and navigate to the holly image. Draw the holly image in your blank file. Rotate and resize the image (using the move tool). Click on Simplify in the Custom Shape toolbar.

2 Select Layer>Duplicate Layer and then flip the new layer horizontally (Image>Rotate>Flip Layer Horizontal). Move the new layer so the two images are "nose-to-nose" and the center berries overlap. Select the Custom Shape tool again and choose the swirl image. Draw it on the screen above the holly. Simplify the shape, then duplicate the layer and flip it vertically.

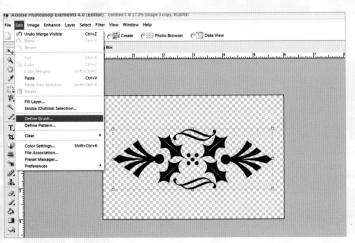

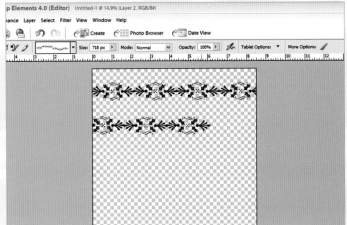

3 Select the Custom Shape tool once more and add a fan-shaped flourish. Simplify the shape, then duplicate it and flip it horizontally. Merge the layers, then select Edit>Define Brush. Name your brush, click OK, and close the file. Open a new 8.5" x 11" (22cm x 28cm) file. Open a new layer, then select a color and click on the brush tool. Click on the fly-out menu and choose Preset Manager. Scroll down to select your new brush, then choose Save Set. Name your brush and click OK. Click Done to exit.

4 Open the More Options menu from the Brush toolbar to adjust the spacing and other settings for your brush. (I changed the spacing to 250 for my brush, but you can experiment with your own design.) Click on the screen to apply your brush. To stamp your image repeatedly in a straight line, hold down the shift button while dragging your mouse across the screen.

Note: When a shape, text or other image is simplified, you can no longer edit the object. Simplification (also called rasterization) is required for tasks such as adding filters to text or custom shapes.

Lesson 3:
Using AutoShapes | Beginner

May Flaum

Program:
Microsoft Word

New technique:
Adding AutoShapes to a
document

Skills you'll need:
Opening the Drawing
toolbar (p. 79)
Resizing images (p. 27)
Inserting WordArt (p. 47)

The playground is a favorite spot for our family, and most of the time, the camera stays behind. On this particular day, I decided to bring it with me so I could record all the fun. To create this page, I inserted AutoShapes and WordArt into a Word document and printed them on cardstock. After cutting, I used a glaze pen to accent the title and let it dry. Then I arranged the title and photos on background paper and adhered them to the page along with the printed embellishments. To complete, I added ribbon, rub-ons, punched stars and brads.

DIGITAL SUPPLIES:
Static font (Two Peas in a Bucket)

TRADITIONAL SUPPLIES:
Patterned paper (American Crafts, KI Memories, Scenic Route); letter stickers, ribbon (American Crafts); rub-on letters (KI Memories); rub-on accents (Heidi Grace); star punch (Fiskars); brads (unknown); pen (Sakura)

Using Word's AutoShapes—like arrows and brackets—can lend a playful look to a layout. Browse through the AutoShapes gallery to see what other looks you can create for your pages.

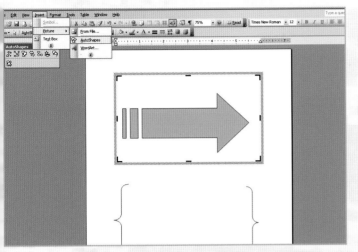

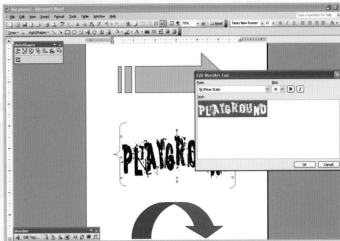

1 Open a new document and go to Insert>Picture> AutoShapes. The AutoShape toolbar will open and you can choose an arrow (or other shape) by clicking on the icons. Edit the color of the arrow using the Drawing toolbar, and edit the arrow's size and shape as needed.

2 Add a pair of brackets and another arrow to your document. Edit them as desired using the Drawing toolbar. Then use WordArt to create a decorative title for the page. Place the title between the brackets.

Another Great Idea!

You can insert other Word AutoShapes to create simple embellishments for your page, like the abstract flowers Audrey created with circles. Insert the shapes, layering the circles and changing the colors. Print and apply dimensional adhesive and brads to your printed embellishments.

DIGITAL SUPPLIES:
Patterned paper by Summer Simmons (Sugar Giggles); A Beautiful Mess font (Two Peas in a Bucket)

TRADITIONAL SUPPLIES:
Patterned paper, transparent frame (My Mind's Eye); brads (Making Memories); corner rounder; ink (Clearsnap); stamps (Purple Onion); clear top coat (Stampin' Up); dimensional paint (Polymark); epoxy accent (Me & My Big Ideas)

Audrey Neal

Lesson 3:
Using AutoShapes | Intermediate

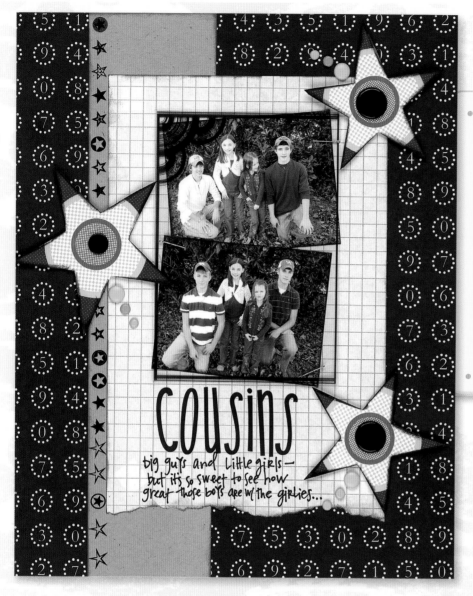

Audrey Neal

Program:
Microsoft Word

New technique:
Applying patterns to AutoShapes

Skills you'll need:
Opening the Drawing toolbar (p. 79)
Inserting AutoShapes (p. 79)
Formatting AutoShapes (p. 79)
Moving images (p. 31)

It's so fun to watch my younger cousins play with my girls. These are tough teenage guys, yet they're so sweet and gentle with the girls. To create this layout, I printed the circles on photo paper and cut them out. Then I traced the star-shaped chipboard on top of the circles, cut them out and mounted the paper stars on the chipboard. I inked the edges and attached the brads to the centers. I added rub-ons to a kraft strip, inked the edges, then adhered them to the background paper. I inked graph paper, ripped the bottom and attached that to the page as well. I printed the photo frame onto a transparency and stapled it over two wallet-sized photos. To finish, I added the stars and yellow brads, then added a title and handwritten journaling.

DIGITAL SUPPLIES:
Frame from Touch of Funk kit by Kim Christensen

TRADITIONAL SUPPLIES:
Cardstock (Bazzill); patterned paper (Scenic Route); rub-on letters and accents (Chatterbox, CherryArte); chipboard stars (Deluxe Designs); brads; ink (Clearsnap); graph paper; transparency; adhesive (Beacon); pen (Sakura)

Take advantage of the number of patterns and textures in Word to create fun chipboard shapes and other embellishments for your layouts.

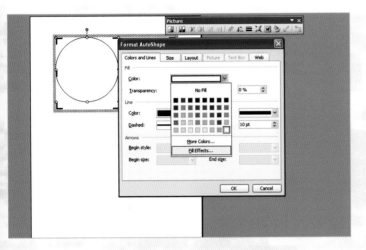

1 Open a new document, and open the Drawing toolbar. Insert a circle and adjust the width to about 3" (8cm). Format the circle in the Format AutoShape menu, increasing the line weight to 10 points and choosing a line color (I used dark blue). Under Fill, select the same color as your line color. Go to Fill>Color>Fill Effects, click on the Pattern tab, and select a pattern.

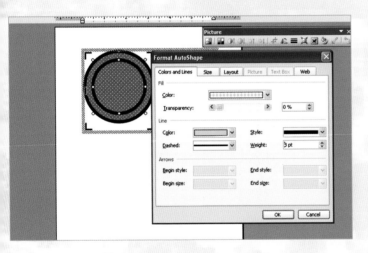

2 Copy and paste your circle. Resize your new circle smaller than the original and move it on top of the larger circle. Format the new circle by changing the line weight, the line and fill colors, and the fill pattern.

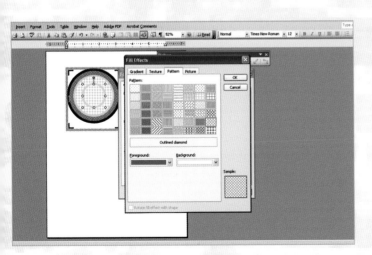

3 Copy and paste another circle, resizing it smaller than the second circle, and move the new circle on top of the other two. Change the new circle's line weight, line color, fill color and fill pattern. Select the three circles, then copy and paste as many embellishments as you need for your page.

Lesson 4:
Combining Images and Custom Shapes | Beginner

Audrey Neal

Program:
Adobe Photoshop Elements

New technique:
Creating a photo collage and embellishment using the Custom Shape tool

Skills you'll need:
Moving images (p. 29)
Using the Custom
Shape tool (p. 95)
Simplifying images (p. 95)
Duplicating layers (p. 95)
Moving images (p. 29)
Selecting layers (p. 35)
Merging select layers (p. 37)
Using the Marquee tool (p. 33)
Clipping layers (p. 37)

Although my youngest daughter is just as likely to run when I pull out the camera, there are times when she actually wants me to take her picture. What she really wants, though, is to make silly faces and then look at herself on the camera screen. (I oblige her, of course.) To create this page, I made a photo collage in Photoshop Elements and printed it onto matte photo paper. I adhered the photos to pink cardstock and a wide strip of patterned paper. Then I printed labels and attached them to chipboard, then printed a tab and attached it to the layout using brads. I embellished the page with flowers, ribbons, brads, rub-ons and rhinestones.

DIGITAL SUPPLIES:
Page template from A Little Eclectic kit by Janet Phillips (Scrapbook Graphics); papers and elements from Aloha kit by Zoe Pearn (Sweet Shoppe Designs)

TRADITIONAL SUPPLIES:
Cardstock (WorldWin); chipboard circle, patterned paper, rub-on accents (Urban Lily); chipboard oval (Deluxe Designs); ribbon (American Crafts, Strano); brads (Paper Studio); rhinestones (Heidi Swapp); flowers (Bazzill, Doodlebug, Heidi Swapp); adhesive (Beacon); pen (Zig)

Are you tired of constantly measuring and cropping your photos to fit them on your layout? Layering basic shapes allows you to fit multiple photos and embellishments on a layout without the hassle.

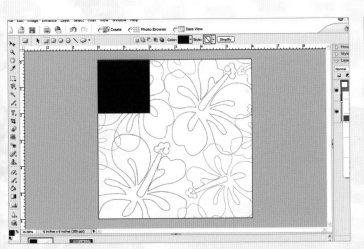

1 Open a new 6" x 6" (15cm x 15cm) file. Open your patterned paper file and drag it onto your blank page. Select the custom shape tool and set it to square. Draw a small square, approximately 2" x 2" (5cm x 5 cm), and then simplify the shape.

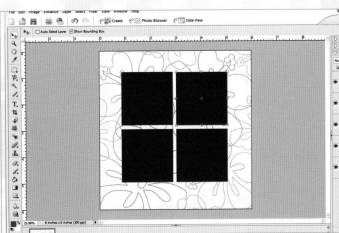

2 Duplicate the layer with the shape three times. Arrange the squares so that there is a small border between them and they are centered on the page.

3 In the Layers palette, select the layer with the square in the top left corner. Open a photo and drag it onto your page. Resize it to fit over the first square layer. Group the photo layer with the square layer (select them and hit <ctrl+G>), and merge the two layers. Repeat the process with the other three squares, adding a new photo to each. Merge the four square layers; do not merge the layers with the background.

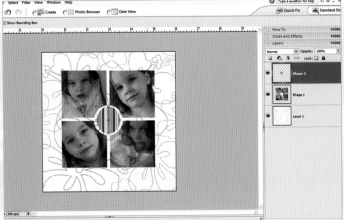

4 Click on the photo layer. Select the Elliptical Marquee tool and draw a circle in the center of the photos. Press the delete button to "cut out" the circle, revealing the patterned paper underneath. Use the Custom Shape tool to draw a smaller circle in the center of the circular cut out, then simplify the shape. Choose a patterned paper (like the striped one I used) and drag it above the circle. Clip the paper to the circle, then merge the layers and flatten the entire image.

Lesson 4:
Combining Images and Custom Shapes | Intermediate

Audrey Neal

Program:
Adobe Photoshop
Elements

New technique:
Adding a photo to text and a
custom shape

Skills you'll need:
Using the Custom
Shape tool (p. 95)
Simplifying images (p. 95)
Resizing images (p. 29)
Moving images (p. 29)
Using the Text tool (p. 33)
Erasing images (p. 35)
Merging select layers (p. 37)
Merging all layers (p. 33)
Selecting layers (p. 35)
Clipping layers (p. 37)

I always come home from our zoo trips with tons of animal photos—they make such perfect photo subjects! Making this layout was an easy way to fit my best photos on one spread. To create the layout, I modified a 12″ x 12″ (30cm x 30cm) page template to fit all my photos along with a journaling box. I also created the sun and zoo image in Photoshop, cutting and pasting some parts of the photo to fill in the blank spots in the image. I printed the photo collage and sun image on cardstock. I made the sun accent and the letters in the word Memphis by using Photoshop to overlay the custom sun shape and the title letters with digital patterned paper, then printed them onto printable shrink sheets.

DIGITAL SUPPLIES:
Papers by Misty Mareda (Twisted Lollipop Shoppe); template by Janet Phillips (Scrapbook Graphics); journaling block by Katie Pertiet (Designer Digitals); AL Hairbrained font (Two Peas in a Bucket)

TRADITIONAL SUPPLIES:
Cardstock (Bazzill); patterned paper (Around the Block); ribbon (Strano); ink; sandpaper; adhesive (Beacon); pen (Zig)

Combining custom shapes with text is a great way to create a unique title. Add a photo to the mix, and you've got yourself a creative design to enhance any layout.

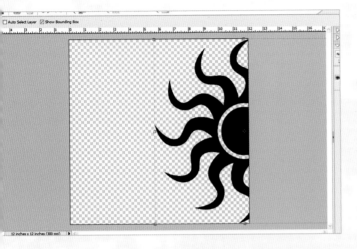

1 Open a new 12″ x 12″ (30cm x 30cm) file. Select the Custom Shape tool and navigate to the sun image. Draw the image on your screen and then simplify the shape. Resize the sun to the height of your file, and place it so that half of the image bleeds outside of the file.

2 Select the Text tool and choose a thick font. Set your point size to 100 or larger (depending on the font style). Type a word from your title and move it over part of the sun. Simplify the text layer. Make sure the sun image is the selected layer and choose the Eraser tool. As needed, erase any part of the sun that shows through the title.

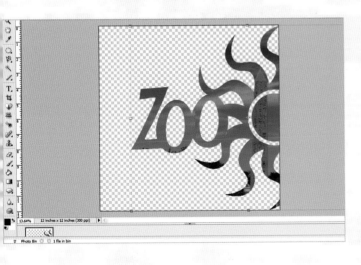

3 Merge the sun layer with the text layer. Open your photo file. Drag the photo into your file and place it above the sun/text layer. Resize the photo so it covers the entire image. Clip the photo layer to the other layer, and then merge the layers when you're finished.

Lesson 5:
Putting It All Together
Beginner/Intermediate

May Flaum

Program:
Microsoft Word

New technique:
Assembling various elements to create a digital layout in Word

Skills you'll need:
Adjusting page orientation (p. 23)
Inserting images (p. 23)
Resizing images (p. 27)
Ordering images (p. 53)
Moving images (p. 31)
Inserting text boxes (p. 47)
Formatting text boxes (p. 45)

To honor our newest pets, I wanted a page that would make a splash. Lucky for me, I had a kit called "Gold Fishie"—perfect! To create this colorful page, I assembled various digital elements—fish, flowers, paper, photo, journaling—and printed the page on 8.5" x 11" (22cm x 28cm) cardstock. I assembled the page by layering various lengths of patterned paper on a piece of cardstock and attaching the printed page on top. I attached the rickrack and sequins using strong glue, then added a tag, rhinestone brad, title stickers and other embellishments. I finished the layout by adding "bubbles" and accenting the title with a black pen.

DIGITAL SUPPLIES:
Paper, images by Katie Pertiet (Designer Digitals); 2Peas Beef Broccoli font (Two Peas in a Bucket)

TRADITIONAL SUPPLIES:
Patterned paper (American Crafts, KI Memories); letter stickers, metal photo corner (American Crafts); photo corner, rub-on accents, tab (KI Memories); epoxy dots (Cloud 9); tag (Heidi Grace); ribbon (May Arts, unknown); brad (Making Memories); pen (Sakura)

Combining your new skills in Word to create a digital layout makes paper scrapbooking really fast! Simply layer your digital elements, print the page and assemble it with a few paper embellishments for a quick and easy layout.

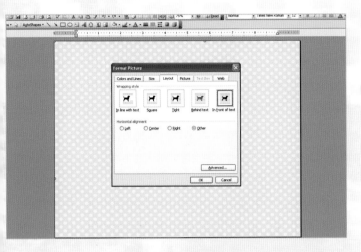

1 Open a new document and change the page orientation to landscape. Insert a patterned paper and resize it to cover the entire page. Then go to the Format Picture menu and click on the Layout tab. Choose the option that says "Behind Text."

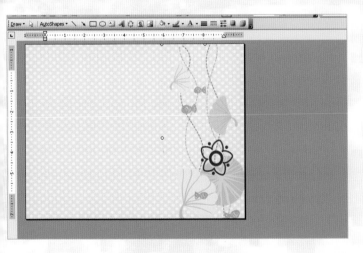

2 Insert a digital embellishment. In the Format Picture menu change the setting to "Behind Text." Then resize the image, move it and adjust any other settings as needed.

3 Insert a photo and additional embellishments following the steps above. Then insert a transparent text box and type your journaling. Make any other necessary adjustments to the layout before printing.

Lesson 5:
Putting It All Together | Advanced

It is one of my simple pleasures. A cup of good tea in the afternoon served in a dainty cup. Of course I usually have a few cups, and enjoy some chocolate or other sweet to go along with it. It might not be as nice as having tea at the Ritz, but I can treat myself to a bit of luxury right here at home.

Afternoon Tea

May Flaum

Program:
Adobe Photoshop Elements

New technique:
Assembling various elements to create a digital layout in Photoshop Elements

Skills you'll need:
Moving images (p. 29)
Resizing images (p. 29)
Adjusting brightness (p. 25)
Using the Text tool (p. 33)
Using the Paint Bucket tool (p. 93)
Opening new layers (p. 37)
Using the Brush tool (p. 35)
Ordering layers (p. 33, 37)

I love capturing life's little moments that I enjoy so much. Almost every afternoon during my daughter's nap time, I enjoy a pot of tea (hot or iced) and some sweets. I had been saving the beautiful doily for a page about tea, and including it on the layout really helped me set the mood for the page. To create this layout, I started by attaching the doily to the background cardstock. Over that, I attached the digital page—the photos, title, journaling, and other digital embellishments printed on cardstock. Then I wove a thin piece of ribbon through wide lace and attached them to the bottom of the page. I edged the printed paper with a gold leafing pen and completed the look with buttons, flowers, brads and other accents.

DIGITAL SUPPLIES:
Paper from Unconditional kit by Jen Wilson 💿; photo frames, stamped block by Katie Pertiet (Designer Digitals); Bohemian font (Two Peas in a Bucket)

TRADITIONAL SUPPLIES:
Cardstock (Prism); flowers, pin (Heidi Grace); brads (K&Co.); stamps (Purple Onion); buttons (Autumn Leaves); lace (Fancy Pants); ribbon (May Arts); gold leafing pen (Krylon)

When you put all your Photoshop skills together to create a page, even a mostly digital layout truly shows off your own unique style.

1 Open a blank file and open your photos and patterned paper. Drag the paper into the blank file. Resize your photos to fit the layout, and drag them into the blank file. Open some decorative frames, adjust their brightness (from black to white) and place them over the photos, resizing them as needed.

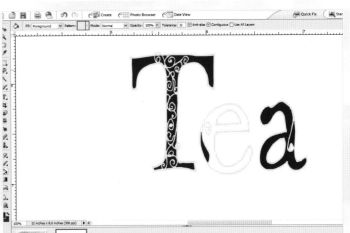

2 Open another blank file and type your title using a decorative outline font. (I used a font decorated with swirls.) Then use the paint bucket tool to fill in the letters with color. Move the title into the file with your patterned paper and resize it as needed.

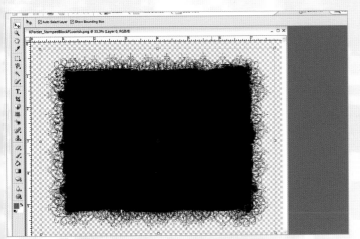

3 Open another file with a stamped block. Use the paint bucket tool to change its color, and drag the image into your other file to create a solid background for your title and journaling.

4 Open a new layer and stamp a flowery brush along the edges of the page. Finally, add journaling over the stamped block. Reorder the layers as needed (e.g., to move the text in front of the brush).

Putting It All Together:
Gallery of Ideas

Now things get even more fun! Once you're comfortable working with your computer program(s), you're ready to mix it up and put your own spin on hybrid scrapbooking. We asked nine designers to share their layouts using both paper and digital elements, including the digital kits included with this book. As you turn the pages of the gallery, you'll get even more ideas, inspiration and eye candy for your journey into the wonderful world of hybrid scrapbooking.

Angela says her son can't resist a cool-looking tool, and he agreed to try sushi just to use the chopsticks. To re-create this page, add a photo and brackets to a digital page in Photoshop. Select the brackets and cover them with another digital paper, clipping the paper to the brackets. (Tip: To add another digital element to your layout, consider scanning chopsticks and adding your journaling digitally over the scanned image.)

Sushi

Angela Daniels

DIGITAL SUPPLIES:
Paper from Perfect Summer kit by Jackie Eckles; brackets from Seriously Pink kit by Poppy Andrews

TRADITIONAL SUPPLIES:
Cardstock (Bazzill); chipboard letters (Li'l Davis); chopsticks; pen

Jackie captured her boys in a candid summer moment running and playing. To reflect the boys' free spirits, she used a carefree approach to her layout. To re-create the page, use Photoshop to type "Perfect Play" over the photo, then add a photo overlay. Print the photo on photo paper. Next, open the digital papers and quotation and assemble them in a blank file. Crop as desired.

Play

Jackie Eckles

DIGITAL SUPPLIES:
Elements from Perfect Summer kit by Jackie Eckles

TRADITIONAL SUPPLIES:
Cardstock, brads (Bazzill); letter stickers (Making Memories); rub-on accents (Creative Imaginations); flowers (Prima); acrylic paint; pen (Zig)

As the title suggests, this page is all about her grandma's silly dog, and Caroline uses fun, bright colors to set the mood. To create a similar page, open a new file in Photoshop and open any other needed files. Type the title text in the new file. Then drag digital paper into the file and place it over the text; select the paper layer and clip it to the title. Add the title to another new file along with the label, papers and photos.

Silly Dog
Caroline Ikeji

DIGITAL SUPPLIES:
Paper from Sweet Baby Chic kit by Michelle Coleman ; label, papers, stripe accent from Touch of Funk kit by Kim Christensen

TRADITIONAL SUPPLIES:
Cardstock (Bazzill); patterned paper (American Crafts, Fancy Pants, Scenic Route); photo corners (American Crafts); buttons (Jo-Ann Stores); rub-on accents (American Crafts); pen

Caroline created this page to pay tribute to a long-distance friend. She customized embellishments by cutting flowers digitally from a patterned paper. To re-create this look, open a new file in Photoshop, and open your digital papers, photos and frame. Cut strips of paper and arrange them along with the photos and frame in the blank file. Then cut out the flowers from a floral paper using the lasso tool. Drag the flowers onto the digital layout, resizing them as needed.

Miss U
Caroline Ikeji

DIGITAL SUPPLIES:
Paper from Seriously Pink kit by Poppy Andrews ; frame from A Touch of Funk kit by Kim Christensen

TRADITIONAL SUPPLIES:
Cardstock (Bazzill); letter stickers, rub-on accents (American Crafts); buttons (Jo-Ann Stores); pen

This page celebrates the biggest source of joy in my life—my family. To re-create this page, open a new Word document, and insert digital papers and embellishments from the Welcome Home kit (including the journaling block, hearts, typed text, flower and tag). Resize and arrange them as desired, overlapping elements to create a dimensional look. Then add a title to the document using WordArt.

Our Family
May Flaum

DIGITAL SUPPLIES:
Papers, flower and journal block from Welcome Home kit by Lynn Grieveson ; hearts and tag from Unconditional kit by Jen Wilson ; journaling circle from Vagabond kit by Jan Crowley

TRADITIONAL SUPPLIES:
Cardstock (Prima); transparency (Hambly); rub-on accents (Heidi Grace); buttons (Autumn Leaves); inks (Ranger); adhesive foam; pen (Sakura)

Resurrection Day
Kathleen Summers

DIGITAL SUPPLIES:
Paper from Sweet Baby Chic kit by Michelle Coleman

TRADITIONAL SUPPLIES:
Cardstock; patterned paper (Chatterbox); stamps (Inque Boutique); buttons (Heidi Grace, unknown); stamping ink (Ranger)

By creating a photo collage, Kathleen was able to share several moments from her family's Easter celebration. To re-create this page, open a digital paper in Word. Type a title (minus the first letter) and journaling in two separate transparent text boxes using white text. Move the text boxes over the digital paper. Then, in a separate document, create a digital collage of your favorite photos.

With just a little floss and some buttons, Amy added texture and dimension to her mostly digital page. To re-create this layout, open a new 8.5" x 11" (22cm x 28cm) file in Photoshop. Then open digital elements from the Perfect Summer kit (papers, doodles, buttons, flowers, frame, stitching, and letters), the photo, and knotted ribbon from the Flowering Horizons kit. Move the digital elements into the blank file and arrange them as desired. Then drag title letters into the file, add journaling using the text tool, and add the ribbon.

Spy I Spy
Amy Martin

DIGITAL SUPPLIES:
Perfect Summer kit by Jackie Eckles; ribbon from Flowering Horizons kit by Katie Pertiet

TRADITIONAL SUPPLIES:
Photo paper, buttons, ribbon (unknown); floss; pen

Photo templates make it easy to assemble several photos from one event on a page. Include digital paper in the collage for added interest. To create a similar layout, open the photo template in Photoshop, and open your photo files and digital paper files. Drag the photos one at a time onto the template, placing them over the appropriate layers and then cropping them into shapes. Cover some spaces with digital patterned paper (dragging them onto the template as you did the photos).

Eggs
May Flaum

DIGITAL SUPPLIES:
Paper from Bloom kit by Tracy Ann Robinson; template from template kit by Janet Phillips

TRADITIONAL SUPPLIES:
Cardstock (Prism); rub-on letters (Mustard Moon); journaling card (My Mind's Eye); ribbon (Making Memories); flowers (Prima); buttons (Doodlebug); brads (Heidi Grace); paint (Ranger); pen (Sakura)

"I don't have anything urban enough!" was my first thought about scrapbooking this photo of my cousin. But digital brushes provide a cool look for the layout. To create a similar page, open your photo in Photoshop, then stamp various graffiti brushes. Add a title and a journaling stamp before printing. Then print the same photo in a 2" x 3" (5cm x 8cm) size, cut it and adhere it to a piece of chipboard.

Sam
May Flaum

DIGITAL SUPPLIES:
Brushes by Jason Gaylor (Designfruit); journal stamp by Katie Pertiet (Designer Digitals); Mechanical Fun, Retro Rock fonts (Internet downloads)

TRADITIONAL SUPPLIES:
Cardstock (Prism); chipboard accents (Deluxe Designs); ribbon (Strano); paint (Jacquard); brads; pens (American Crafts, Sakura)

After realizing I didn't have a paper file folder to use on my layout, I decorated a digital one. To re-create the look, open a plain digital file folder in Photoshop. Select a flourish brush and stamp it at 50 percent opacity over the file folder. Move a photo into the file, placing it over the folder, then add a photo frame. Add another frame for journaling and type your title. In a separate file, add a digital frame to the other photos before printing.

Violet
May Flaum

DIGITAL SUPPLIES:
Brushes, file folder, frame and journal accents by Katie Pertiet (Designer Digitals); Santa's Sleigh, Scriptina fonts (Internet downloads)

TRADITIONAL SUPPLIES:
Patterned paper, twill tape (Imagination Project); ribbon (Cloud 9, May Arts); stamps (Art DeClassified); epoxy sticker (K&Co.); decorative scissors; buttons, lace (unknown); thread; stamping ink; pen (Sakura)

Sporting events make up a big part of the McKeehan family's daily life. To re-create Wendy's grungy title and photo borders, begin by opening each photo in Photoshop and placing a photo frame over them; allow room for a white border to print. (The edges were inked by hand.) Add small text to one photo before printing. In a new document, type a large, bold title, and print it on a transparency for dimension.

Play Hard or Go Home!
Wendy McKeehan

DIGITAL SUPPLIES:
Paper from Perfect Summer kit by Jackie Eckles 👀 ; letters by Katie Pertiet (Designer Digitals); frames from Authentic Me kit by Lauren Reid 👀 ; HullunKruunu font (Internet download)

TRADITIONAL SUPPLIES:
Patterned paper, rub-on accents (Scenic Route); transparency; watermark ink; adhesive

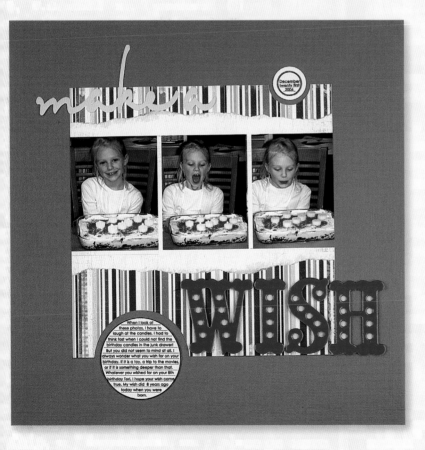

Birthdays are special events, but it's easy to fall into a rut when scrapbooking them year after year. Although simple, Wendy's design mixes it up a bit. To re-create this look in Photoshop, insert photos over a strip of torn digital paper, then layer those pieces over a digital patterned paper. Type journaling onto digital tags before printing. To create a guide for hand-cut lettering, type your title backwards and print it onto the back of a sheet of colored cardstock.

Make a Wish!
Wendy McKeehan

DIGITAL SUPPLIES:
Striped template by Kellie Mize (Designer Digitals); papers by Anna Aspnes, Dana Zarling and Katie Pertiet (Designer Digitals); paper tears by Anna Aspnes (Designer Digitals); circle stamps from Vagabond kit by Jan Crowley 👀 ; Century Gothic font (Microsoft); Eight Fifteen font (Internet download)

TRADITIONAL SUPPLIES:
Cardstock (WorldWin); chipboard letters (Li'l Davis); circle punches; adhesive

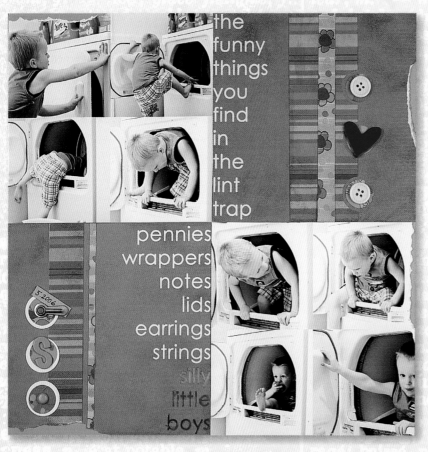

Jennifer's layout made us laugh out loud when we saw it! We love that she was able to capture one of childhood's silly sides. To re-create the digital elements, start by cropping photos (in Word or Photoshop) to 3" x 3" (8cm x 8cm) and arrange them into two 6" x 6" (15cm x 15cm) square collages. In a new document, create two more 6" x 6" (15cm x 15cm) squares with text and digital papers. Then insert strips of other digital papers into a blank document and print.

Silly Little Boys

Jennifer Olson

DIGITAL SUPPLIES:
Papers from Perfect Summer kit by Jackie Eckles 💿; Century Gothic font (Microsoft)

TRADITIONAL SUPPLIES:
Cardstock (Bazzill); chipboard letter and heart (Heidi Swapp); photo turns (7gypsies); brads; clear topcoat (Stampin' Up); buttons (unknown)

Being able to capture a moment in time is one of the joys of scrapbooking, as Katrina discovered with this photo of her son. To copy these digital techniques, begin by re-coloring the background paper to match your photo, using Photoshop's eye dropper tool to select a color from the photo. Layer the photo and other digital papers, then add a digital seal with a slight shadow for dimension. Finally, print an overlay on a transparency.

A10

Katrina Simeck

DIGITAL SUPPLIES:
Patterned papers, overlay and seal from Authentic Me kit by Lauren Reid 💿

TRADITIONAL SUPPLIES:
Cardstock (Bazzill); wooden letter (Li'l Davis); number tag, rub-on accent (American Crafts); transparency; brads; adhesive

Linda used a transparency to mimic the reflection of the mirror that so enamored her son. To create a similar layout, assemble strips of patterned paper, journaling and a title onto one Photoshop file. Draw various colors from the patterned paper to create a multi-colored title. Then print a digital grid onto a transparency (and attach with two strips of machine stitching). Edit the digital photos as needed before printing them.

Vain
Linda Barber

DIGITAL SUPPLIES:
Green and striped papers from Seriously Pink kit by Poppy Andrews ; orange paper and grid from Touch of Funk kit by Kim Christensen

TRADITIONAL SUPPLIES:
Cardstock (Bazzill); transparency; photo paper; thread

Linda's reflective layout captures the questions that seldom occur to those in their twenties. The punched square is backed with a pink transparency, symbolizing a peek through rose-colored glasses. The three holes in the orange block represent a peek into reality. To create a page like this one, add a line of white text along the left edge of a photo in Photoshop before printing it. In another file, re-color two digital papers and add the title text and journaling to the page. Then print a pink-hued digital paper on a transparency.

Peek
Linda Barber

DIGITAL SUPPLIES:
Green paper from Authentic Me kit by Lauren Reid ; orange and pink papers from Flowering Horizons kit by Katie Pertiet

TRADITIONAL SUPPLIES:
Cardstock (Bazzill)

Cathy turns things around with this interesting take on a two-page layout, using a landscape rather than a portrait orientation. To make a page like this one, use Word to create the title and subtitle in colors that match those of the digital flowers. Then repeat rows of additional words (summer, loving and fun in the sun) in the same three colors and punch a circle from each after printing. Print the digital flowers to add to the page.

Summer Loving
Cathy Pascual

DIGITAL SUPPLIES:
Flowers from Perfect Summer kit by Jackie Eckles ●●; Bauhaus 93, Geosanslight fonts (Internet downloads) corner rounder; chalk ink; pen

TRADITIONAL SUPPLIES:
Cardstock (Bazzill); Kraft cardstock; patterned paper (American Crafts); letter stickers (Making Memories); sticker accents (Around the Block); ribbon, rickrack (Beaux Regards); corner rounder; chalk ink; pen

Anyone with small children can probably relate to the guessing game Cathy plays with her daughter's artwork. A digital template helped Cathy pull this design together. To re-create this page, start by opening the sketch template in Photoshop to put a preliminary version of the layout together, cropping photos to fit the template. Then print the digital pieces separately. Print the title, journaling and bird stamp on white cardstock, and print the photos on photo paper. Finally, print the patterned paper and circle embellishment.

Is It a Bird?
Cathy Pascual

DIGITAL SUPPLIES:
Paper, bird stamp, circle sticker from Touch of Funk kit by Kim Christensen ●●; template from template kit by Jen Caputo ●●; Century Schoolbook font (Microsoft); Waterfalls font (Internet download)

TRADITIONAL SUPPLIES:
Cardstock (Bazzill, DMD); ink; staples

Cathy used the decorative text in the Authentic Me kit as her starting point for this introspective layout. To re-create this page, insert the decorative text over the digital lined paper in Word or Photoshop and print. Open another digital paper in Photoshop and place a photo over it. Open the curved text path on top of both layers and add journaling. Change the font color of the journaling as needed for definition and readability. Print it as one element and create swirls when cutting.

Perhaps
Cathy Pascual

DIGITAL SUPPLIES:
Paper, rolodex card, decorative text from Authentic Me kit by Lauren Reid ⊙; text path from template kit by Jen Caputo ⊙; Verdana font (Microsoft)

TRADITIONAL SUPPLIES:
Cardstock (Bazzill); patterned paper (American Crafts, Scenic Route); chipboard stars (Scrapworks); rub-on stitches (Die Cuts With A View); chalk ink; rhinestone border (Heidi Swapp); ribbon (Beaux Regards); pen

Cliché
Audrey Neal

DIGITAL SUPPLIES:
Heart, swirls, tag, decorative text from Unconditional kit by Jen Wilson ⊙; AL Modern Type font (Two Peas in a Bucket); Eight Fifteen font (Internet download); Garamond font (Microsoft)

TRADITIONAL SUPPLIES:
Frame, journaling square, patterned papers (My Mind's Eye); adhesive foam; pen (Sakura)

I love that digital embellishments allow me to add layers without sacrificing space in albums. To re-create this page, start by moving the digital tag in the Unconditional kit into a new Photoshop file and placing the bracket and swirls over it. Then use the kit alphabet to create the word *cliché*. Use the text tool to write the word "truth" seven times. In another layer, type "truth" in a large script font, simplify the layer, reduce its opacity, then add a stroke. Finally, type "the truth is never a" and place the phrase as needed.

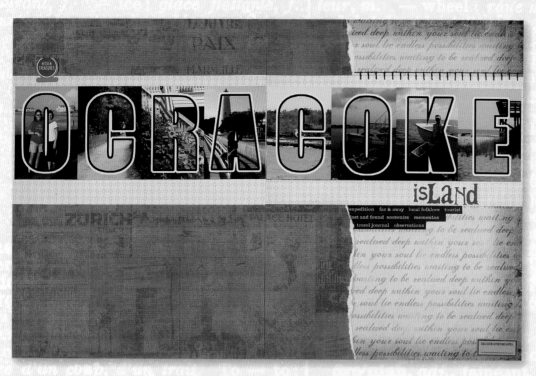

Ocracoke Island
Audrey Neal

DIGITAL SUPPLIES:
Green paper from Vagabond kit by Jan Crowley 💿; script paper from Authentic Me kit by Lauren Reid 💿; Impact font (Microsoft)

TRADITIONAL SUPPLIES:
Patterned paper (Scenic Route); rub-on letters (Fancy Pants); rub-on stitches (Adornit); sticker accents (7gypsies)

Combine a blocky page title with a series of dual-toned photographs for a graphic opening statement to a vacation album. To re-create this effect, open a 24" x 17" (61cm x 43cm) document in Photoshop and arrange the photos across the page. Merge the photo layers and then duplicate them. Remove the color from the bottom layer. Add the title, centering each letter over one photo. Merge the colored photo layer with the letters, then add two strokes to the letters' edges.

This page captures Jaren's enthusiasm by highlighting the photo of his fist in the air. To re-create the look, use Photoshop's eraser tool to erase the background of your main photo, leaving just the subject. Make additional, careful swipes with the eraser to delete the background as close as possible to the subject. Then layer a large strip of digital paper and squares of other papers, and place the photos over the paper, making sure your main photo is on top. Add a drop shadow to each layer. Finally, print additional pieces of digital paper and embellishments from the kit.

Total Playground Domination
Audrey Neal

DIGITAL SUPPLIES:
Papers, bullseye, die-cut, tab from Touch of Funk kit by Kim Christensen 💿

TRADITIONAL SUPPLIES:
Cardstock (Bazzill); chipboard letters (Heidi Swapp); stamps (Hampton Art, Purple Onion); ink (Clearsnap); star brad (unknown); pen (Sakura); adhesive (Beacon)

Photo by Natalie Braxton

Sometimes the subtlest details are the most stunning, such as this large photo of my husband blended with the patterned paper. To re-create this effect, open a digital paper file in Photoshop. Open a photo and resize it to fit your layout, then place it on the layer above the paper. Change the blend mode to overlay and reduce the opacity until you're satisfied with it. For the appearance of additional texture, add a digital tear and a second layer of paper before printing.

Quite Simply

Audrey Neal

DIGITAL SUPPLIES:
Cardboard, paper tear by Tracy Ann Robinson (Scrapbook Bytes); frame, heart, rolodex card, striped paper from Authentic Me kit by Lauren Reid

TRADITIONAL SUPPLIES:
Cardstock (WorldWin); chipboard letters (Heidi Swapp); word stickers (Magnetic Poetry); fabric tag (7gypsies); ink; pen (Sakura)

Still One Minute

Audrey Neal

DIGITAL SUPPLIES:
Trebuchet font (Microsoft)

TRADITIONAL SUPPLIES:
Patterned paper, rub-on accents (Paper Salon); letter stamps (Purple Onion); ink; brad; corner rounder; adhesive (Beacon)

Photo by Kim Hendricks

For me, these pictures capture the time when a mother finds herself torn between wanting kids to stay tiny but wanting them to gain independence. To re-create this layout, start by inserting a long text box into a Word document and typing in white text (to make the border). Use AutoShape circles to create scallops. Create a second text box, type repeated journaling in white, and then type additional journaling in larger blue font. Print digital photos to add to the page.

about the contributing artists

Linda Barber is a wife, mother of three and a storyteller. She's also a cook, boo-boo kisser and (maybe someday) a world traveler. She's loved crafting since she was a little kid. These days, she creates slightly less mess with slightly more sophisticated supplies, but it's still for the same reasons: to make art, to express herself and to tell a story.

Angela Daniels fell in love with scrapbooking when she first walked into a scrapbook store and has been an avid scrapbooker ever since. Adding a computer obsession to her traditional scrapbooking has been a match made in heaven. She enjoys sharing her passion for scrapbooking on the daily Internet show, *Scrapbook Lifestyle*, and also does work for several design teams. When she's not scrapbooking, she can be found spending time with her two children.

Caroline Ikeji is a college student living in southern California. She has been scrapbooking for about two years and has worked on numerous design teams and been published in various magazines and books. She is also a 2008 Memory Makers Master. When she's not studying or scrapbooking, Caroline loves to read, eat, shop, write and spend time with those she loves the most.

Amy Martin has been digital scrapbooking since 2004, and she loves the challenge of trying new styles, while enjoying preserving family memories. When she's not scrapbooking she can be found spending time with her husband and three children. She also enjoys swimming, running and reading.

Wendy McKeehan has been involved in the scrapbooking industry for more than nine years. She has done everything from demonstrating to teaching to layout design, and her work can be found in a number of publications. When she's not capturing the moment, she's singing in the church choir and attending her kids' school, music and sports activities.

Jennifer Olson has been scrapbooking with paper for nine years and scrapbooking digitally for almost three. She's a work-at-home mom to three active children and wife to one crazy man. Her proudest scrapbooking moment was being chosen as one of *Creating Keepsakes'* Hall of Fame winners in 2006. She also enjoys reading, knitting and playing Spiderman with her son.

Cathy Pascual is a stay-at-home mom and self-proclaimed full-time scrapbooker. Frequently published, she enjoys all forms of scrapbooking, from paper to digital to hybrid, as long as she's expressing herself through her photographs and pages. She lives in the Northwest with her husband, Jamie, and two-year-old daughter, Sofia.

Katrina Simeck was introduced to scrapbooking at a home party almost 10 years ago. Initially overwhelmed with the rules, she scrapped on and off before fully immersing herself in the hobby a few years later. She loves that scrapbooking offers a creative outlet for a crazed life. When she's not in her scrap room, she's spending time with her husband Rob, 15-year-old Hope, and 10-year-old Austin.

Until **Kathleen Summers** started scrapbooking a few years ago, she didn't feel she had a creative bone in her body. Now she has been published in numerous idea books and magazines, and she loves all variations of the art form, whether she's using her stash of scrapbooking supplies or her computer. Kathleen lives in Northern California with her husband and two children.

about the digital kit designers

Poppy Andrews is a wife, mother and artist who works almost full time outside of the home. She lives in New Jersey with her family and has close to seven years experience with graphic design. Originally a paper scrapbooker, Poppy was introduced to digital scrapbooking through a friend and was instantly hooked. She started designing her own supplies in 2005 and started selling her work in 2006. She enjoys traveling, reading, art, good movies, music, a good laugh, her two cats and her family.

An engineer by day, **Jen Caputo** lives in the Chicago area with her two cats. She met digital scrapbooking in the summer of 2005 and fell in love instantly. That fall, she began creating Digital Layered Sketch Templates and soon found there was quite a demand for her templates. Jen sells her digital page templates online at Scrapbook Graphics.
www.jencaputo.typepad.com

Michelle Coleman started scrapping digitally in December 2004 and designing digital product in March 2005. She currently designs products for Fancy Pants Designs and is the owner and

designer of Little Dreamer Designs. Michelle is also a contributing editor for Memory Makers Magazine, and her work has been widely published. The mother of two beautiful girls, when she isn't designing, she can be found playing Barbie dolls and Little Mermaid, and scrapbooking her memories.
www.littledreamerdesigns.com

Although **Kim Christensen** was once one of those people who assumed they'd never be able to scrapbook, she soon discovered that digital scrapbooking was the perfect tool for channeling her creativity. Her inspiration comes from her wonderful family of four children under seven and a devoted husband. A country girl with a love of gardens and chickens, her life is her muse and she finds that each day brings new, exciting tidbits to both scrap about and use for design inspiration.
www.scrapartist.com

In 2003, with two small children and a teeny apartment, **Jan Crowley** discovered that digital scrapbooking just made more sense. After many changes, a new baby, and trying to find her design groove, Jan decided to give her designs away for free. With Meredith Fenwick, Jan launched Songbird Avenue, a Web site whose profits are donated to different charities every month.
www.songbirdavenue.com

A mother of two and a long-time scrapbooker, **Jackie Eckles** loves preserving every memory possible in her scrapbook pages. In September 2004, she discovered digital and now creates for Little Dreamer Designs and is being published in numerous magazines and books.
www.littledreamerdesigns.com

Lynn Grieveson began scrapbooking in 2002 and then switched to digital scrapbooking in 2004. Now a published artist and accomplished designer, she creates her designs and layouts from her home office in New Zealand where she lives with her husband and two daughters.
www.lynngrieveson.typepad.com

After being a professional graphic designer for more than 20 years, **Katie Pertiet** followed her scrapbooking obsession to a career change. In 2005, she started Designer Digitals and started focusing on product development for scrapbooking. When she's not working, Katie can be found spending time with her family or scrapbooking her many memories.
www.designerdigitals.com

Janet Phillips started digital scrapbooking in 2005 after reading an article in a scrapping magazine. By 2006, Janet had started creating and selling digital scrapbooking templates in a wide range of styles. In 2007, Janet started to experiment with traditional and hybrid scrapping and now finds great enjoyment in all different kinds of scrapping. A work at home mom to three preschool children, she also cares for at-risk children with her husband in their home in the Orlando area. Her digital products can be found at Scrapbook Graphics.
www.phillipsfamily.typepad.com/janet

A wife and mother of three, **Lauren Reid** began designing digitally in early 2006, after a long love of traditional scrapbooking. In her scrap world, paper and digital is the perfect marriage because she has her beloved "undo" button in Photoshop, while keeping the satisfaction of real ink on her fingers. Her digital products can be found online at Oscraps.
www.laurenreiddesigns.com/blog

Tracy Ann Robinson left a lengthy career in sales and marketing to become a stay-at-home mum when her daughter was three. She lives in Melbourne, Australia, with her daughter, Jemma, and her husband of 17 years, Graeme. Discovering in her forties that she has a creative side and an artist within has been one of the most rewarding journeys of her life. Her digital designs can be found at Tracy Ann Digital Art.
www.tracyanndigitalart.com

Jen Wilson lives in Ontario, Canada, with her husband, two children and house full of animal friends. Jen enjoys simple things like going to the park, hitting the library, hopping around town as an amateur photographer and making time for many art projects and a cup of coffee! Soon after discovering digital scrapbooking, she began designing—one of her true passions and very rewarding for her.
www.jenwilsondesigns.com

source guide

The following companies manufacture products featured in this book. Please check your local retailers to find these materials, or go to a company's Web site for the latest product releases. In addition, we have made every attempt to properly credit the items mentioned in this book. We apologize to any company that we have listed incorrectly, and we would appreciate hearing from you.

3M
(800) 364-3577
www.3m.com

7gypsies
(877) 749-7797
www.sevengypsies.com

Adobe Systems Incorporated
(800) 833-6687
www.adobe.com

Adornit/Carolee's Creations
(435) 563-1100
www.adornit.com

American Crafts
(801) 226-0747
www.americancrafts.com

Around the Block
(801) 593-1946
www.aroundtheblockproducts.com

Art Declassified
www.artdeclassified.com

Autumn Leaves
(800) 588-6707
www.autumnleaves.com

BasicGrey
(801) 544-1116
www.basicgrey.com

Bazzill Basics Paper
(480) 558-8557
www.bazzillbasics.com

Beacon Adhesives
(914) 699-3405
www.beaconcreates.com

Beaux Regards
(203) 438-1105
www.beauxregards.com

Chatterbox, Inc.
(888) 416-6260
www.chatterboxinc.com

CherryArte
(212) 465-3495
www.cherryarte.com

Clearsnap, Inc.
(888) 448-4862
www.clearsnap.com

Cloud 9 Design
(866) 348-5661
www.cloud9design.biz

Colorbox - see Clearsnap

Creative Imaginations
(800) 942-6487
www.cigift.com

Daisy D's Paper Company
(888) 601-8955
www.daisydspaper.com

Delta Technical Coatings, Inc.
(800) 423-4135
www.deltacrafts.com

Deluxe Designs
(480) 497-9005
www.deluxecuts.com

Design by Dani
www.designbydani.com/store

Designer Digitals
www.designerdigitals.com

Designfruit
www.designfruit.com

Die Cuts With A View
(801) 224-6766
www.diecutswithaview.com

Digital Design Essentials
www.digitaldesignessentials.com

DMD Industries, Inc.
(800) 727-2727
www.dmdind.com

Doodlebug Design Inc.
(877) 800-9190
www.doodlebug.ws

Dream Street Papers
(480) 275-9736
www.dreamstreetpapers.com

Fancy Pants Designs, LLC
(801) 779-3212
www.fancypantsdesigns.com

Fiskars, Inc.
(866) 348-5661
www.fiskars.com

Fontwerks
(604) 942-3105
www.fontwerks.com

Grafix
(800) 447-2349
www.grafixarts.com

Hambly Studios
(800) 451-3999
www.hamblystudios.com

Hampton Art Stamps, Inc.
(800) 229-1019
www.hamptonart.com

Heidi Grace Designs, Inc.
(866) 348-5661
www.heidigrace.com

Heidi Swapp/Advantus Corporation
(904) 482-0092
www.heidiswapp.com

Imagination Project, Inc.
(888) 477-6532
www.imaginationproject.com

Inque Boutique Inc.
www.inqueboutique.com

Jaquard Products/Rupert, Gibbon & Spider, Inc.
(800) 442-0455
www.jacquardproducts.com

Jo-Ann Stores
www.joann.com

Junkitz
732) 792-1108
www.junkitz.com

K&Company
888) 244-2083
www.kandcompany.com

KI Memories
972) 243-5595
www.kimemories.com

Krylon
800) 457-9566
www.krylon.com

Li'l Davis Designs
480) 223-0080
www.lildavisdesigns.com

Little Dreamer Designs
www.littledreamerdesigns.com

Luxe Designs
972) 573-2120
www.luxedesigns.com

Magnetic Poetry
800) 370-7697
www.magneticpoetry.com

Making Memories
801) 294-0430
www.makingmemories.com

May Arts
800) 442-3950
www.mayarts.com

me & my BiG ideas
949) 583-2065
www.meandmybigideas.com

Melissa Frances/Heart & Home, Inc.
888) 616-6166
www.melissafrances.com

Microsoft Corporation
www.microsoft.com

Mustard Moon
(763) 493-5157
www.mustardmoon.com

My Digital Muse
www.mydigitalmuse.com

My Mind's Eye, Inc.
(800) 665-5116
www.mymindseye.com

Nunn Design

(800) 761-3557
www.nunndesign.com

Office Depot
www.officedepot.com

Paper Salon
(800) 627-2648
www.papersalon.com

Paper Studio
(480) 557-5700
www.paperstudio.com

Piggy Tales
(702) 755-8600
www.piggytales.com

Polymark/Polymer Marketing, Inc.
(770) 952-1147
www.polymark.com

Prima Marketing, Inc.
(909) 627-5532
www.primamarketinginc.com

Prism Papers
(866) 902-1002
www.prismpapers.com

Provo Craft
(800) 937-7686
www.provocraft.com

Purple Onion Designs
www.purpleoniondesigns.com

Ranger Industries, Inc.
(800) 244-2211
www.rangerink.com

Sakura Hobby Craft
(310) 212-7878
www.sakuracraft.com

Scenic Route Paper Co.
(801) 225-5754
www.scenicroutepaper.com

ScrapArtist
(734) 717-7775
www.scrapartist.com

Scrapbook-Bytes
(607) 642-5391
www.scrapbook-bytes.com

Scrapbook Graphics
www.scrapbookgraphics.com

Scrapworks, LLC/As You Wish

Products, LLC
(801) 363-1010
www.scrapworks.com

Stampin' Up!
(800) 782-6787
www.stampinup.com

StazOn - see Tsukineko

Strano Designs
(508) 454-4615
www.stranodesigns.com

Sugar Giggles
www.sugargiggles.com

Sugarloaf Products, Inc.
(770) 484-0722
www.sugarloafproducts.com

Sweet Shoppe Designs
www.sweetshoppedesigns.com

Technique Tuesday, LLC
(503) 644-4073
www.techniquetuesday.com

Therm O Web, Inc.
(800) 323-0799
www.thermoweb.com

Tsukineko, Inc.
(800) 769-6633
www.tsukineko.com

Twisted Lollipop
www.twistedlollipop.com

Two Peas in a Bucket
(888) 896-7327
www.twopeasinabucket.com

Uniball/Sanford
(800) 323-0749
www.uniball-na.com

Urban Lily
www.urbanlily.com

WorldWin Papers
(888) 834-6455
www.worldwinpapers.com

Zig/Kuretake Co. Ltd.
www.kuretake.co/jp

*index

Type Cast
Learn fresh, creative uses for a variety of type treatments, as well expert tips on composing attention-getting titles and getting into the flow of journaling.
ISBN-13: 978-1-59963-003-8
ISBN-10: 1-59963-003-6
paperback
128 pages
Z0695

The Scrapbook Designer's Workbook
Join author Kari Hansen as she takes the fear out of understanding and using design principles to create fabulous scrapbook layouts.
ISBN-13: 978-1-892127-95-2
ISBN-10: 1-892127-95-4
hardcover with enclosed spiral
128 pages
Z0533

Find Your Groove
Kitty Foster and Wendy McKeehan take you on a journey to discovering your own groovy scrapbook style through quizzes, exercises, challenges and page after page of fabulous layouts sure to inspire.
ISBN-13: 978-1-59963-006-9
ISBN-10: 1-59963-006-0
paperback
112 pages
Z0787

Focal Point
Discover unique and stunning ways to showcase your favorite photos with these fresh and fabulous altering and transfer techniques.
ISBN-13: 978-1-892127-96-9
ISBN-10: 1-892127-96-2
paperback
128 pages
Z0530